S
Dropshipping Guide

How to build a $100K per Month Online Business in 2019. Combine Dropshipping, Affiliate Marketing, Email Marketing & Facebook Advertising into 1 Massive E-Commerce Business

Written By

Marcus Rogers

purposes only. All effort has been executed to present accurate, up to date, and reliable, complete information. No warranties of any kind are declared or implied. Readers acknowledge that the author is not engaging in the rendering of legal, financial, medical or professional advice. The content within this book has been derived from various sources. Please consult a licensed professional before attempting any techniques outlined in this book.

By reading this document, the reader agrees that under no circumstances is the author responsible for any losses, direct or indirect, which are incurred as a result of the use of information contained within this document, including, but not limited to, — errors, omissions, or inaccuracies.

Table Of Contents

Introduction

Starting a business is not an easy feat. In fact, it can seem quite overwhelming and even scary. Since you have made up your mind about starting a business, I want to congratulate you for taking this first step. There are several benefits of being an entrepreneur and you can enjoy all these benefits, provided you know what you need to do. You must not be under any misconception about the effort and time it takes to launch and maintain a successful business. You must be willing to dedicate your time and energy to build and nurture your business. If you think you can launch a business and become successful overnight, you need to revisit this idea once again.

If you want to start a dropshipping business, then this is the perfect book for you.

In this book, you will learn everything that you need to know about successfully launching your dropshipping business. Dropshipping is a lucrative business idea and in this book, you will learn about building a dropshipping business using Shopify, about affiliate marketing, email marketing, and Facebook advertising to start a successful e-commerce business.

I want to thank you for choosing this book. If you are ready to learn more about the world of dropshipping and everything related to it, then there is no time like the present! So, let us get started immediately.

Chapter 1: The Overview of a Business Model

If you want to establish a successful business, then you need a great business model. A business model acts as a blueprint and provides you with a brief overview of the different aspects of your business. In this section, you will learn about the brief overview of different aspects of a business model that you can use to create a successful and profitable online business.

Dropshipping

Dropshipping is a business model of supply chain management where retailers don't have to maintain or manage their inventory. They can promote the products of their suppliers and earn a handsome commission for doing so. A dropshipper is essentially an intermediary between suppliers and customers. The dropshipper will transfer the order information to the supplier while holding onto a certain portion of the payment received, as commission and the supplier will directly dispatch the product from the warehouse to the customer.

In the dropshipping model of business, the parties involved include the supplier, a dropshipping store, and the customers. The customers will order the product from the dropshipping store. The store will then transfer the details of the order to the supplier along with customer information. The supplier will then directly ship the product to the customer. The dropshipping store will always sell the product at a higher price than the cost of acquisition and that's their profit margin. For instance, if the wholesale rate of a product is $150, then the dropshipping store can sell the same product for $200 and so the profit that you make as a dropshipper is $50!

As a dropshipper, there are a couple of aspects of the business that you need to understand. You have the power to decide the price of the products. If you want to start wholesaling your product, then you can do so without partnering with other manufacturers by using services like AliExpress, eBay, Amazon, or even Shopify. The final aspect of the business that you need to understand is that you will earn through arbitrage.

Pros and Cons of Dropshipping

Well, dropshipping is certainly a lucrative business model, but here is a list of the different benefits it offers that make dropshipping more appealing.

Easy to Enter

As a dropshipper, you don't have to pay upfront for the inventory. You only need to pay fees for hosting and your domain. Since there is no inventory, loss of revenue is highly unlikely. You have the option of upselling your products.

Convenience

Dropshipping is quite convenient for the dropshipper as well as the supplier. The dropshipper doesn't have to worry about shipping or packaging the product. The supplier doesn't have to worry about marketing and other promotional activities. As a dropshipper, you also have the option of working with various wholesalers simultaneously.

Scale and Remodel

Since your business model is fully digitized, you don't need to worry about storage facilities, and it makes dropshipping an easy business model to scale. Even if one product doesn't sell well on your dropshipping store, you have the option of moving onto better products.

Less Risk

It is quite inexpensive to start a dropshipping store. All that you need is a domain and a hosting service, and you can get started immediately. The risk involved in this form of business is quite low.

Dropshipping is a lucrative business model, especially with the different benefits it offers. It doesn't mean that there aren't any drawbacks for this business model. If you want to start a business, it is important that you are aware of the benefits as well as the drawbacks it must optimize your business. Here are a couple of drawbacks of the dropshipping model.

High Competition

Competition is prevalent in all walks of life and e-commerce stores are no exception. As a store owner, you must strive to stand out from the crowd by providing high-quality and unique products to your customers. High competition proves that the niche you selected is profitable, but it can be a thorn in your side if you aren't careful. New stores keep popping up almost every day and you need to make your store stand out from those of your competitors.

Low Margins

Dropshipping isn't a short-term business idea. If you want to be a successful dropshipper, then you must be in it for the long run. It is all about staying in the game and steadily making your way up the ladder. You must come up with a method to increase your profit margin. Instead of selling ten units per day, try to sell about 50 or so to increase your profits. A great thing about dropshipping is that you don't have to worry about logistics, so you can work on scaling your business.

Full Liability

As a dropshipper, it is quite probable that you might end up selling a product that you have never seen. Therefore, the chances of the product not living up to the consumer's expectations can be quite high. If the customer is not satisfied with the product, then the liability rests on you to process the refund and return the product to the supplier, so you must take some time and create a perfectly understandable and unambiguous return policy for your business.

Managing Orders

One aspect of the business that most fledgling dropshippers struggle with is when the demand for their product increases rapidly. You need to manage all the orders that fly in and you must not let it overwhelm you.

Shopify

Now that you know what dropshipping is about, the next step is to learn about Shopify. In this book, you will learn about setting up a dropshipping business with Shopify. Before you learn about starting your business, you must understand the platform that you are going to use.

Shopify is a cloud-based shopping cart option. For a monthly fee, it gives you access to an administrative panel that lets you store data, add products, and process the orders you receive. It also offers several free and paid-for design templates for your online store. The themes available are quite clean and modern. Also,

Shopify offers different editing tools that you can use to create a theme that suits your brand well. When you subscribe to Shopify, it also offers secure and reliable hosting for your dropshipping website. You don't have to worry about any technical issues like the site crashing or getting hacked.

Also, Shopify provides great 24/7-customer support. Whenever you find yourself in trouble or anything like that, you can immediately contact the customer support. For a dropshipper, Shopify is the perfect option for everything they need.

Pros and Cons

Easy to Use

Shopify is quite easy to use, and you don't have to be tech-savvy to use this platform. It is quite simple to add products and process bulk orders. The web design is user-friendly, and the editing tools are simple to use.

Cost-Effective

The startup cost on Shopify is quite low and the monthly fees payable are certainly affordable. The basic plan costs about $29 per month and the mid-level plan will cost you $79 per month. You must select a plan that meets your needs.

Themes

As a merchant on Shopify, you can choose from a vast array of themes that are free and are adapted for mobile use. There are free and paid-for options to choose from.

Shopify is the go-to destination for a lot of dropshippers because of its integration with Ordoro and Oberlo.

Support

The technical support team on Shopify is available at any time and you can reach them through your phone, live chat, or even email. There are various self-help options available as well. There are no business hours applicable for the customer support team and they are available 24/7.

There has been a significant increase in the client load on Shopify and their support team is finding it difficult to keep up with this increased demand. The customer support service might not always be as quick as you hope for.

Functionality

There are various pre-set features that a merchant will need while setting up a store on Shopify; however, there will be times when a business might have a specific requirement and Shopify might not have the necessary features to accommodate those needs. This problem can be easily fixed if you purchase some add-ons. The add-ons certainly make your life easier, but they aren't free and are expensive. This can increase your monthly fees payable.

Transaction Fee

Most online shopping carts have reduced their shopping fees, but according to the pricing plan you opt for, you will need to pay a 0.2 to 0.5% as transaction fees on Shopify.

Email Marketing

Once you set up a store on Shopify, your work doesn't end. In fact, as the owner of an e-commerce store, your work has only just begun. You need to work on marketing and promoting your business. One of the best ways in which you can market your online business is through email marketing. It is the best channel that you can employ to engage in a one-on-one conversations with your existing and potential customers.

Especially in a business like dropshipping, it is important that you not just acquire, but also retain your customers. Why do you need email marketing for your dropshipping business?

Targeted Marketing

With email marketing, you have the option to target specific segments of the customer market. You will initially work with fewer products during the initial phase of your dropshipping business. If you have fewer products to work with, then you need to make sure that you target a specific audience. For instance, if you notice that some customers add products to their cart but don't make a purchase on your website, then you need to target such customers in your subsequent email marketing campaign. You can target such customers by offering them a discount or any other attractive offer to compel them to make a purchase. You can design a specific email marketing campaign to target all those customers who have made a purchase and encourage them to become repeat customers.

Measurable and Data-Driven

Knowledge is power when it comes to email marketing. There are various metrics that you can obtain from your email marketing campaign to design your other marketing strategies. For instance, you can obtain metrics like the click-through rate, open rate, opt-out rate, and so on. These different parameters will help you organize or reorganize your marketing efforts to optimize your marketing campaigns.

Traffic and Sales

Sales are the primary priority for any e-commerce business owner. In a dropshipping business, you must work on increasing the traffic to your site if you want to increase your sales. The best way to do this is by mailing your product catalog to your target audience. If you implement email marketing properly, you can derive exceptional results and increase your sales.

Affordable

Email marketing is perhaps the most affordable method of marketing these days. Apart from the initial start-up and implementation costs, there is hardly any other maintenance cost involved with this method of marketing. You can reach a huge audience quite easily and it will not burn a hole in your pocket. For instance, if you use MailChimp, you can send about 12,000 emails every month for free! So, you need to select a business plan and an email service that will suit your needs.

Omnipresent

Almost everyone has at least one email address these days. Most e-commerce businesses require an email address of the user for signing up and this coupled with the exponential rise in the popularity of online shopping, all online shoppers have at least one email address, so it is safe to say that emails are an omnipresent form of communication. You will learn about the different email marketing strategies that you can employ to grow your email list and successfully sell to your list in the coming chapters.

Affiliate Marketing

Affiliate marketing is a phrase that you might have stumbled across online. There are tens of thousands of articles telling you why you must be minting money with affiliate marketing, and you might feel a little left out if your bank account isn't clocking up cash while you are sleeping. What exactly is affiliate marketing and how can you make use of it for generating a steady stream of passive income for yourself? To put it simply, affiliate marketing is the process of promoting or selling someone else's product or service. You earn a commission on any of the sales made or click-through to a given affiliate site. Doesn't that sound quite simple? In theory, you can have a website without any products or services of your own. It can be a blog, an online journal, or anything similar to it. As long as there is some relation with the product or the service, you are set. Maintaining a website costs money and with affiliate marketing, you can cover all those costs and earn more money. It doesn't cost the owner anything to sign up for an affiliate program and the business owner doesn't have to pay anything until he makes a sale, so it is a win-win situation for both the parties involved.

In this book, you will learn about affiliate marketing, the benefits it offers, about selecting an affiliate program, and the different strategies that you can use to generate income from affiliate marketing.

Selling a product can be difficult, even more so when you aren't able to reach out to your target audience. You might at times need to opt for other means of selling your product. On the other hand, you might need some extra money. In cases like these, both the parties can use affiliate marketing. In simple terms, in affiliate marketing, the vendor can sell their products or services by making use of an affiliate. The affiliate will be responsible for marketing the products to potential customers, allowing the vendor to make a sale, and in turn, the vendor will pay the affiliate for all the effort that they have put in to make that sale. The founder of PC Flowers & Gifts, William J. Tobin, is responsible for creating the concept of affiliate marketing. They made use of Prodigy network for increasing their sales and in turn paid Prodigy Network for the services they offered. You might not have realized it yet, but affiliate marketing is quite prevalent. The simplest form of affiliate marketing can be writing a review of products or services posted on any form of media and the Internet. Making use of the Internet for affiliate marketing has become an increasingly popular practice these days. Companies like Amazon have managed to create their own affiliate program and it has been developing since it was launched in 1996. It is a common practice these days and it is an easy way to earn money, when done properly.

Strategies to Use

Here are a couple of strategies that you can make use of.

A YouTube channel or a Blog Reviewing Products

Blogs provide their readers with useful reviews, articles, and product reviews. Whenever a potential client searches for a product or service he or she is interested in, they can find the reviews on your blog, purchase the product or service by following the affiliate link on your blog, and you will be paid a commission for the sale. It is not easy to create an audience base and it takes considerable time and effort to create a blog that others will want to follow. You can improve your visibility in search engine rankings by creating a YouTube account and by posting videos pertaining to product reviews. You can post the affiliate links to the products you reviewed in the description box.

Promotion and review on your YouTube video or blog

You can make money through affiliate marketing by promoting or reviewing products or services on YouTube or blog. Reviewing products or services is easier than to create new blog posts from scratch. Each blog posts created builds the authority of your blog in the search engine and drives more traffic to your blog. Sharing a product, event program, or seminar can also be promoted on your blog or YouTube channel.

Promoting Products and Services to your Email Listing.

When visitors visit your blog and read your blog articles, a lot of them will end up clicking the affiliate links of products or services you recommend on your blog, which will earn you money. If there is a product or service that you want to share with your followers, sending out an e-mail regarding the recommendation is the best option; however, in promoting products to your email listing, keep in mind these two important rules to follow:

Never recommend or promote a product you have not used personally or feel comfortable using. Think about your followers and if you want them to stay loyal to you, then you must think of their needs as well. Maintain equilibrium between quality and value. Don't bombard your followers with a lot of emails. After all, you don't want to start spamming them, do you? You must be able to provide your customers with content that provides some value to them.

Benefits of Affiliate Marketing

Affiliate marketing not only complements but is also being used as a replacement for the more conventional marketing strategies these days. In affiliate marketing, you don't have to spend time, effort, or finances on creating a new product or service. You simply have to provide a platform that other vendors can make use of for selling their products and services. Let us take a look at all the different benefits that affiliate marketing offers.

Endless Possibilities

One of the easiest ways to start your home-based company is to take up affiliate marketing. As such, there is no limit on the income that you can earn from affiliate marketing. Also, affiliate marketing is considered a low-risk business model.

It is convenient

With affiliate marketing, you have the option of working at your convenience. You are your boss and are therefore in charge of your working hours. When you work for someone else, you are always bound by their rules. There might be times when you need to push your working hours to meet a deadline. With affiliate marketing, you can forget about all this and set your working hours according to your needs and your lifestyle.

You can Track Your Progress

It is quite easy to track the metrics to check your progress with affiliate marketing. You can track the number of people who you are reaching out to, the products that you sold directly or indirectly, and also the profits you are raking in.

Autonomy to Select the Products and Projects

You have complete autonomy to select the products or projects you want to be an affiliate marketer for. You can opt for those products that interest you. You don't have to take up things that you aren't passionate about and can do something that you enjoy.

Work from Anywhere

As an affiliate marketer, you will not have a fixed workplace or working hours. You can pretty much work from anywhere in the world as long as you have a laptop and a reliable Internet connection. You can work according to your convenience and can instead focus on doing the things that you enjoy.

Steady Cash Flow

One of the prominent advantages of becoming an affiliate marketer is that it helps you generate a steady cash flow. You will certainly receive a paycheck even if you work for someone, but you will need to follow the rules and regulations that your employer sets. With affiliate marketing, you are your boss and can work according to your convenience and still earn a steady income. You can also retain your regular job and use affiliate marketing to generate some additional income for yourself.

Facebook Ads

Social media is an integral part of the marketing campaigns for most businesses these days. It is a great way to build an audience, increase engagement, and share content. If you don't want to miss out on reaching a large audience, then you need to use Facebook ads. Facebook is amongst the most popular social media platforms these days and it is a great place for marketing.

Here are the different reasons why you must use Facebook ads in your marketing campaign.

Affordable

You can decide your advertising budget on Facebook. Not just that, you can also set when you want Facebook to start and stop showing the ads. The higher your budget, the greater your reach. In fact, Facebook ads have a great ROI and it is one thing that all marketers will unanimously agree upon. It works well for B2B as well as B2C companies.

Audience

On average, people tend to spend about 40 minutes on Facebook. Apart from that, more than 2 billion people have Facebook accounts and about 1.55 billion users access the platform every month, so it is quite safe to say that most of your target audience is active on Facebook.

Target Users

Facebook provides a lot of information about the people active on this platform. Facebook ads help you target audiences who are most likely to engage with your brand or business. This platform allows you to target your audience according to different criteria like their age, gender, location, job profile, usual behavior, interests, and various other parameters. You also have the option of targeting lookalike audiences on Facebook. It means that you can specifically target those users who are quite similar to your existing audience.

Retargeting

You don't just specifically target a certain audience, but you also have the option of retargeting your audience. It means that you can target all those people who have visited your website in the past, have used your app, or have shared their email address with you. It is quite likely that those who are familiar with your business will be repeat customers.

Easy to use

It is quite easy to set up an advertising campaign on Facebook. You need to select the type of ad you want to run, define your target audience, select a budget and set your timeframe. Facebook ads offer a high degree of customizability and there are multiple formats to choose from. You not only have the option of choosing a pay-per-click model, but you can also opt for a pay per impression, like or action campaigns as well. You will learn more about setting up and running a successful ad campaign on Facebook in the coming chapters.

Analytics

Advertising on Facebook provides you the opportunity to reach various users regardless of whether they are in a buying frame of mind or not. It is not a limitation, but an effective opportunity to gather data. Your ads might not be effective for closing a sale, but they will certainly help increase awareness for your business and capture leads. Facebook provides a lot of information that you can use to analyze your marketing campaign and make it more effective. You can use different metrics like reach, frequency, likes, or impressions you receive to calculate the ROI of your ads. These real-time metrics come in handy if you want to increase the efficiency and the effectiveness of your marketing campaign.

Custom Button

Most digital ads come with a call-to-action button that leads the viewer to a landing page. It is quite effective because it helps the user gather more information about a specific product before they make a decision. If you use Facebook ads, you have the option to customize the call-to-action button to include different actions that are beneficial for your e-commerce website like "contact us, apply now, purchase now," and so on.

Video ads

We live in a world where the rules of advertising and marketing are undergoing a massive overhaul. Video ads are the latest trend in the field of marketing and it is here to stay. Facebook allows you to create video ads that help grab the attention of the viewer.

If you want to increase the reach of your brand on social media, then Facebook is your go-to option. Facebook ads help increase the awareness of your business, attract and nurture leads, and help convert existing users into loyal customers!

Google AdWords

In 2016, Google AdWords generated revenue of over $70 billion. This metric certainly shows that a lot of people are using Google AdWords because it is quite effective. Google AdWords is an online advertising platform that helps advertisers display ads, product listings, video content, and the like for a fee.

AdWords is an advertising service that businesses can use to display their ads on Google and its related advertising network. AdWords is a program that lets the businesses set a budget for advertising and you only need to pay when your target audience views the ad. The primary focus of this service is on keywords. If you use AdWords, then you can create relevant ads by using the keywords that people usually use to search for your business, niche, or industry on Google. Whenever the user types in the relevant keyword, then your ad will be shown next to the search results. The ads are usually shown under the heading "Sponsored Links" on the Google results.

Here are the different reasons why you must include Google AdWords in your marketing strategy.

No Minimum Investment

If you have a limited budget or are just getting started with online marketing, then you must include Google AdWords. In fact, it isn't just small businesses that use this service, but even the large and well-established businesses as well. Even if you have a huge marketing budget, it always makes sense to play it a little safe, at least initially, before you decide to try newer channels. With this option, there is no minimum investment you need to make or fix a monthly advertising budget. It means that the risk involved in this form of advertising is low compared to other options that require an upfront payment. Some keywords do cost more than the others, but if you use the keywords wisely, you can make a dent in the market.

Results

This ad service is affordable, and you need to pay only when you get the results. It is similar to a pay-per-click advertisement wherein you will have to pay only when someone clicks on the specific link. If you set up your advertising campaign properly and incorporate the relevant and negative keywords, then the clicks that you pay for will mostly be for good future prospects and potential clients for your business. You can also use AdWords for retargeting all those users who might have clicked on your ad in the past but aren't your customers yet, it is a great way to generate leads for your dropshipping business.

Good Timing

Whenever someone searches for something in Google, it is quite likely that they are looking for something specific in that moment. Google AdWords gives the business the perfect opportunity to market to their future prospects at the moment when they are considering a buying decision or are thinking about making a purchase. Before the advent of digital marketing and advertising, businesses used to list their services in telephone directories under a category that is similar to or related to their business. Think of Google AdWords as the modern-day telephone directory or register.

Placement

It isn't just timing that matters, but even the locality matters as well. If your ads are being shown to those customers who live beyond the places that you can deliver to, then it doesn't make any sense to invest in such advertisements. Google AdWords also helps with geographical targeting.

Engaging the Customers

When it comes to content marketing, videos are the most effective means of doing this. Research shows that a significant percentage of users are likely to buy a product after they watch an online ad for it. Did you know that Google AdWords manages YouTube advertising as well? It means that if you use Google AdWords, you have an opportunity to get your ads on YouTube videos that are related to your business or products.

SEO

Search Engine Optimization or SEO is quite

important if you want to generate traffic to your website or you want to increase the online visibility of your online business. When you start using important keywords for your AdWords campaign, then the same keywords can be used in your SEO strategy as well to improve the online visibility of your website.

ROI Tracking

Google AdWords helps you track your ROI. It is quite easy to set up and track. You can track web form submissions, e-commerce sales, and even any phone calls made or received. Also, the data that you gather will help you measure the effectiveness of the keywords and ads that are ushering in most of your sales and you can accordingly tweak your marketing budget. If you want to start a business that will help you earn more than 100K in a month, then you need a brilliant business plan. To create a brilliant business plan, you need to make sure that you include the different concepts mentioned in this chapter in your business model.

Chapter 2: Getting Started

Now that you are aware of the different aspects of your business model, the next step is to get started with setting up your online business. Taking the first step is the most difficult aspect of setting up a business. Give yourself a pat on the back for doing this! Now, you need to concentrate on setting up your online business to realize your financial goals.

In this section, you will learn about setting up your online business on Shopify, use ClickBank for affiliate marketing, steps to set up an email marketing campaign, and creating a Facebook ads account.

Set up Shopify Dropshipping Store

In this section, you will learn about all the different steps that you need to follow to create your dropshipping store on Shopify.

Name

The first step is that you must decide on a name for your Shopify dropshipping store. Here are a couple of things that you can keep in mind while selecting a name for the store. The name needs to be simple, easy to pronounce and remember, it needs to be creative and it must be unique. You can use Oberlo's Business name generator to come up with a name for your Shopify store. You will be shown a list of business names and you can select one that appeals to you. Once you come up with a store name, you need to check whether the name is available or not. A simple Google search will help you determine whether a name is available or not.

Shopify Account

It is quite easy to create an account on Shopify for your dropshipping business. You need to visit the homepage of Shopify and you will notice an empty field towards the top of the screen and you need to enter your email address there. Once you enter your email address, it will prompt you to create a password for your account and enter the name that you have finalized for your store. Next, you will need to fill in a couple of details about any previous experience with e-commerce and a couple of other personal details. Once you fill all this in, your Shopify account is up and running. The next step is to configure the settings to successfully launch your dropshipping account

Optimize the Settings

There are a couple of different settings that you need to optimize your Shopify account. You need to go through these instructions carefully because it relates to your store policies, mode of payment, and the shipping rates.

The first thing that you need to do is add a payment option to your store. If you don't add a payment option, then you will not be able to receive payments from customers. To do this, you need to go to the Settings section and click on the Payments tab and add the payment information you want to include. One of the best modes of payment is PayPal, so please don't forget to include this option in your payment section.

Now that you are launching your dropshipping store on Shopify; you need to include necessary store policies. Shopify has a couple of standardized policies for privacy, refunds, and other terms of service for your store. Go to the Settings menu and click on the "Checkout" option and you will find all the above-mentioned fields on the page. Once you are satisfied with the terms of service, you need to click on "Generate" to get started.

As a dropshipper, you need to have clear policies about shipping. The easiest shipping option is to offer free shipping. If you offer different shipping rates according to the regions, then it can be quite confusing for the buyer, so it is a better idea to incorporate the cost of shipping into the price of the products you offer, so if you are offering a product for $20, instead offer it for $25 and provide free shipping. The words "free shipping" can motivate the customer to make a purchase! Go to the "Shipping" tab in the Settings menu and decide your shipping policies.

Launch your Store

Once you add all the necessary information, the next step is to launch your Shopify store. To do this, you need to click on the "Sales Channels" tab in the Settings menu and opt for the "add an online store" option. Once you do this, your Shopify dropshipping store is up and running.

Design the Store

The design of your e-commerce store is as important as the façade of a brick and mortar store. The way you present your store and your brand is quite critical. The store needs to be aesthetically pleasing and must attract the viewers. When it comes to design, there are two primary things that you need to focus on and they are the theme of your store and the logo you opt for.

Shopify offers a range of built-in themes for the store. You can find free as well as paid-for themes on Shopify, so go through the different themes available and select one that best suits your needs and budget. You need a logo for your store so that the customers can identify your brand. Creating a logo might sound like a tough job, but you don't have to be a tech-wiz to get this job done. You can always hire a graphic designer to help you with it. If you don't want to do this, then you can try Oberlo's free online logo maker to create a logo for your brand. If you want to design your own logo, then you can use different software like Photoshop or Canva. You can easily hire a professional to do this work for you from different freelance websites like Upwork or Fiverr.

Use Oberlo

Once you select the designs for your Shopify store, you need to start adding different products so that you can earn some money. To add products that you want to dropship, you must install Oberlo. Oberlo is the leading application for e-commerce store owners who want to import products to their dropshipping stores on Shopify. Oberlo and Shopify offer great integration and you can import and offer high-quality products within no time to your customers.

Once you install Oberlo, you must add a new category to your Shopify store. You can name this category according to the products that you want to sell. If you plan to start an online t-shirt business, then you can name it "clothes" or "t-shirts." Now, you can use Oberlo to search for all the products that you might want to sell. You merely need to click on the import button on the products that you want to include in your product list and all these products will be directly imported to your dropshipping store on Shopify.

You might wonder why you need to use Oberlo. Using Oberlo is a good idea because it provides you access to three types of suppliers and they are the Oberlo suppliers, Oberlo Verified suppliers, and the AliExpress suppliers. If you want to find reliable suppliers easily, then you must explore this option.

Make a Sale

Now that your dropshipping store is up and running on Shopify, the only thing that's left to do is make your first sale. You need to think about generating revenue and to do this, you need to make sales. There are different marketing channels that you can use to direct traffic to your dropshipping store like Facebook ads, Google AdWords, and email marketing. You will learn more about all this in the coming sections.

Affiliate Marketing with ClickBank

So, how can you become an affiliate marketer? There are various ways in which you can generate traffic, build your website, and select products to promote, so which method must you choose? What will work and how do you get started?

Take a deep breath, because you don't have to worry about all this anymore. In this book, you will learn about all the different steps and tips that you need to follow to become a successful affiliate marketer. Affiliate marketing is quite easy, low-risk, and doesn't cost you much.

What is ClickBank? ClickBank is a marketplace for physical and digital goods. It is quite similar to Amazon and it has a great global presence, offers secure payment options, effective tracking options, and is a great platform for affiliate marketers. In this section, you will learn about using ClickBank to become an affiliate marketer.

Step One: Find Products

You need to find at least ten products that interest you and that you want to promote as an affiliate marketer. A great thing about using ClickBank for affiliate marketing is that there are tens of thousands of products to choose from. Once you create a ClickBank account, you need to go to the Marketplace and search for different products that interest you. Make a list of these products as you continue to search for different options. Ideally, save this list in the form of a text file on your laptop or computer for future use.

Step Two: Keywords

The next step is to search for different potential keywords with the help of Google's keyword resource. To do this, you must visit Google's external keyword tool. For all the products that you selected in the previous step, you need to enter the generic keyword that you think is suitable to your product. For instance, if you want to promote a product that cures tinnitus, then the keyword that you will search for is Tinnitus and click on the Get Keywords Ideas option. Go to the "Match Type" drop-down menu and select the option "Phrase Match." You can sort this list according to the global search volume. Once you do this, you must make a list of the relevant keywords that get about 10,000 to 30,000 searches per month. Repeat this process for all the products that you chose in the previous step and you must have ten different lists with you. It is likely that a couple of these lists might be empty since not every keyword will be relevant to you. You need to be patient and don't get discouraged.

Step Three: SEO

Now, you need to check if it is possible for the keywords that you opted for to improve your ranking on Google to increase traffic to your website. Open the Google search engine and type the keywords you gathered in the previous section in the search tab. For instance, if a keyword that you gathered in the previous step is "cure tinnitus" then the phrase that you will search for on Google will be "cure tinnitus." Once you do this, Google will display the search results along with the words "Results 1-10 of about xyz" on the right side. If the xyz number is less than 100,000 then you can move on to the next step. If it is less than 100,000 then you can strike this keyword off your list.

Once you do this, you need to do another Google search and you need to type "inurl:the keyword phrase." For instance, if the keyword you are searching for is cure tinnitus, then type "inurl:cure tinnitus" and look at the results you obtain. If the number is less than 1,250 for the keyword, then it is a keeper. Repeat these steps for all the keywords you gathered in the previous step.

Step Four: Select Keywords

You need to select the keyword that you want, and you need to create a blog on BlogSpot. There are two reasons why you must opt for BlogSpot: it is easy to start a blog and the visibility of these blogs in Google search engine ranking is quite good. You must opt for a keyword with the highest search volume, the least competition numbers from the previous step, and that seems like the best fit for someone who wants to buy your product. There are no right or wrong answers here and you must pick something that meets all these three criteria.

You need to create your blog on BlogSpot, sign up

and start creating content for your posts. While you are setting up a blog, please make sure that the blog's title includes your chosen keyword. Add certain characters to the keyword to make sure that it is unique. This blog will help you increase the awareness about your business and increase sales. You can also add images of the product that you are promoting as an affiliate marketer to the blog. While you are creating content about the products, don't add any fictional information. Don't overexaggerate the benefits of the product and try to be as honest as possible. You need to give a truthful and realistic description of the products if you want happy and satisfied customers for your business.

Step Five: Link building

The key to SEO is by link building and it's also the best way to increase your visibility in the search engine results for the keywords that you want to use. You must work on creating at least 5 to 10 backlinks daily. The idea is quite simple; you must get a link to your website, use the keyword of your choice in the description, and then use the keyword as an "anchor text" (the clickable text that leads you to the actual site) whenever you possibly can.

Follow these simple steps to start using ClickBank to become a successful affiliate marketer.

Email Marketing

Email marketing is a brilliant technique to market your business. You can improve the rate of conversion by emailing your customers with personalized offers. The cost of email marketing is quite low when you compare it to any of the other methods of marketing. For instance, Adore Me has a brilliant strategy for their email marketing campaigns. The subject lines, the content they use along with the visuals are all carefully thought out. A couple of subject lines that they used for their email marketing campaigns include "Drop everything. Your customized picks are waiting for you" to "you are on the list." Each of their emails is carefully crafted and encourages the reader to take some favorable action. Here are a couple of tips that can help you with email marketing.

You have probably received a ton of e-commerce emails. Why did you ever open such an email? Why did you click on the links in the emails? Perhaps the subject line caught your attention, maybe you were curious about what the email was all about, or perhaps the topic discussed was quite interesting. Email marketing is all about trial and error, so it is quite likely that you will need to test a couple of different layouts until you find something that the customer will enjoy. You can send out an email with a product list, one with good content on an interesting topic related to your niche, or it can even be a strategic combination of content and product lists.

You need to be creative when you are building your email list. You can send a quiz to the readers that will provide them a personalized recommendation at the end of the quiz. You can even host a contest or a giveaway; this by itself is a great marketing tool.

You need to segment your email list so that you can send different offers according to the preferences of your audience. You must always acknowledge and reward your loyal customers. To do this you can send them certain exclusive deals or exclusive access to your products. You need to create email subject lines that will encourage the viewer to click on the email and read through it. You will learn about growing your email list and marketing products to your email list in the coming chapters.

Before you learn about all that, you must acquaint yourself with a couple of email marketing tools that will come in handy.

Soundest allows you to send up to 15,000 emails per month and up to 2000 emails per day. This is a great tool if you have a small budget or a small email list. To increase the sales of your store, you can create campaign boosters and other welcome emails that will help establish a relationship with your customers. The other email platforms that you can use include Wheelio, Privy, and Better Coupon Box. Email marketing is essential if you want to grow your dropshipping business and increase your sales.

Facebook Advertising

Why do you need another account when you might already have a Facebook account? If you have a Facebook ad account, it helps increase the precision of your advertising campaign on Facebook. If you create an ad account, it helps you set an account through the Business Manager account, so what is a Facebook ad account? It helps you manage ads on this platform and several people can manage it. How can you create this account? Follow the simple steps given in this section to create your Facebook ads account.

The first step is to log into your Facebook Business Manager account, go to the Settings and click on the Ad Account option.

Once you do this, add the account name and link

it to an advertising profile. You need to select your method of payment, your time zone, and the currency.

You can add other users who can manage this account on your behalf. If you don't have any other users in your business manager account, then you can add users to your business manager account and then use them for your ad account. If you are the only one who uses the business manager account, then you can skip this step since you don't need to add anyone. If you click on the "Add a person" option, then the popup window will ask you to add the information about the other person you want to include. Include the necessary information and assign a role of analyst or administrator to that person.

You need to continue and save your changes so that you can check the various advertising features it offers. You will need to set up a method of payment after this and that's about it. You need to enter your payment details and you can get started. If you don't want to add your payment details immediately, you can always do this after. You will have access to the targeting and audience settings, but you cannot run your campaign until you fill in the payment details.

Tips for Dropshipping

Well, it's quite amazing that you want to be a dropshipper. Now that you want to be a dropshipper, there are a couple of simple tips that you must keep in mind to improve your business. In this section, you will learn about the different tips to become a successful dropshipper.

Work on Marketing

You have the option of automating different aspects of a dropshipping business these days. Whenever you automate your business, then you have the time to focus on important aspects of business such as branding and marketing. It can be quite fun to design the logo, create content, design the graphics, and such, but if you want to start making a profit, then you need to concentrate on marketing your dropshipping business. You must spend some time on learning about the way that ads work, increase the traffic to your site, and work on converting the visitors to your store into paying customers.

When it comes to increasing your web traffic, there are two strategies that work best and these are SEO and ads. You must remember that the usual rate of conversion for an e-commerce store is around 1-2%, so if you have less than 100 visitors, then you will not be able to be profitable. The higher the traffic, the higher the rate of conversion. Usually, dropshippers tend to focus only on ads. Ads are certainly helpful if you are looking to produce instant results and increase your sales immediately, but they are effective only for a while. If you want to constantly drive up your sales in the long run, then you must focus on your SEO strategies.

SEO not only improves your rankings on search engines, but it also improves your online visibility. You can make sure that your cost of acquisition stays low while you reach a greater audience with a minimal budget, if you create blog content and start to optimize your product pages.

Not just your product pages, but you must also optimize your website for conversions. If you want to compel people to make a purchase, then you need to remember that the two factors that increase the chances of a sale are scarcity and urgency. To optimize your dropshipping website, you must increase the chances of impulse buying and add some positive customer testimonials to make the website seem credible and more appealing.

Amazing Offer

You need to create a compelling offer. You must try hard to not end up like those store owners who fail to include any offers or sales on their products. At times, a visitor needs an initial push or a slight shove to make a purchase. By offering sales or bundles you offer the necessary motivation the buyer needs to make a purchase. If you manage to present a good product with a great deal, then your rate of conversion will certainly increase.

Another offer that seems to do rather well in dropshipping is a bundle deal. Whenever you decide to create a bundle deal, you must focus on selling more units of a specific product. For instance, if you want to dropship hair extensions, then a bundle will include more hair extensions than a single unit. If your audience likes this product, then they will certainly want more of it. Here comes the tricky part: you must not only encourage the visitor to purchase something, but you must try to upsell it. Well, a combo offer always seems more appealing than a single unit.

Don't Underprice

There are a couple of platforms that allow you to underprice a product. You will be able to earn a profit if the cost of the goods you procure is reasonably close to the wholesale price and you can sell your products at market value. The aim of a dropshipping business like any other business is to be profitable. If a product costs you $5, then you need to ensure that you sell it for at least more than $15 if you want to be profitable. Don't ever underprice your products. You must consider all the aspects of business like the cost of goods, marketing expenses, and any other business expenses while pricing a product.

You must not undercut your prices because other dropshippers are doing so. You needn't worry about undercutting the prices as long as you make sure that the price you are charging is fair and well within the market value. If you want to earn a higher return on your orders, then you must strive to increase the average value of an order.

Quality Suppliers

You will need a supplier who is reliable, offers good products, is easy to work with, and is punctual with deliveries. At times, you will come across suppliers who don't offer any of these things. While selecting a supplier, you must thoroughly vet the supplier. As a dropshipper, your rate of success is directly proportional to the supplier you work with. You will learn about finding the right supplier in the coming chapters.

Automate your Business

If you use dropshipping tools like Oberlo or Shopify, then you can automate several aspects of your business. Even if you have a full-time job or want to generate passive income, then you must come up with different ways in which you can automate your business. When you automate your business, you can free up your time and concentrate on things that do matter. There are several e-commerce tools you can use to automate, grow, and even scale your business operations. For instance, you can use Buffer to automate the posts on social media and Kit helps you automate several marketing activities like retargeting, email marketing, and even advertising.

A Presentable Website

An important aspect of a dropshipping business is your business website. The website you create must be customer-friendly and must be easy to use. The website needs to appeal to customers. Your website is as important as the physical façade of a retail store. A lot of new dropshippers don't spend sufficient time designing an appealing website. Your website is an extension of your business, so you need to include important features like a well-defined product list, important images, as well as placeholder text. Before you can launch your store, you can look at the websites of your competitors or other dropshippers in your niche for inspiration. What do their websites look like and what do they include on their homepage? Are the websites easy to navigate? Do they include their logos or images on the website? What are the different pages their websites have? What are the things that are lacking and what can you do better?

After you look at a couple of other websites, you

will have a general idea of all the things that are good and bad for your business. You can imitate those aspects of their business that appeal to you and change the ones that you don't like. Your dropshipping business's website is critical for your success as a dropshipper. Your website must appeal to the viewer and it must encourage them to make a purchase.

Don't Forget about Your Competition

An important thing that you must never forget about is your competition. This tip applies to all businesses including dropshipping. You must update yourself on the strategies and marketing efforts that your competitors are making and keep a track of their scalability as well. In fact, to do this, you simply need to follow them on different social media platforms. If you do this, you can not only keep track of their business but can also track and measure their progress. Also, it will give you some ideas about the things that you can include in your marketing strategies. Doing this will help you gauge the profitability of a specific product, its demand, as well as its popularity amongst the audience. If you start paying attention to these simple details, you can improve the efficiency and the effectiveness of your business. The best way to progress is to look at what others are doing and learn from their mistakes.

Trustworthy Brand

It is your responsibility to ensure that your business does well, and you are the only one that can ensure it. You represent your business, so you need to put your best foot forward. If you work on strengthening the positioning of your brand, then you can strengthen your reputation as a leader in your niche. You must look at different aspects of your business that set you apart from your competitors. Make a list of the various aspects of the business that you can leverage to improve the identity of your business. You must concentrate on building trust for your business; you must work on building your brand's awareness and identity amongst your target audience.

Follow these simple tips and you will be able to launch a successful dropshipping business. You will learn more about all these aspects of dropshipping in the coming chapters.

Chapter 3: Product Research

Product research is critical to the success of your business. You must select a great product if you want to create a business that will help you earn more than 100k per month. To select the perfect product for your dropshipping business, you need to spend some time on research.

There are three important things that you need to keep in mind while selecting a product for your dropshipping business. The product that you opt for needs to be profitable, it needs to have good demand, and it must be easy to ship. If the product that you opt for meets all three requirements, then you are off to a good start. Research is a critical aspect while you are searching for the best dropshipping products for your business. You need to immerse yourself in the virtual world of online businesses, go through different marketplaces like eBay, Amazon or AliExpress. You need to understand the product trends, the sellers who are active in a given niche, the profit margins, seller fees, and the shipping costs. If you already have a list of potential products that you can use for your dropshipping business, then you can test them with the criterion that is discussed in this chapter.

Brainstorm

If you have a list of products that you think will be good for your dropshipping business, then that's great. If you don't, then you don't have to worry.

It might seem like a basic step, but it is quite important. When you are thinking about all the different products that you can dropship, you might start to wonder if a specific product might sell online. You need to make a list of all the products that you think will sell online. At times these ideas might pop into your mind when you are thinking about a product that might solve a problem you are facing in your life. You can also get product ideas when you interact with others.

Before you can select a great dropshipping product, you need to take some time and think about all the different ideas for products that might be floating around in your head. Even if the idea seems ridiculous initially, please make a list of the product ideas. You must also acquaint yourself with the products that are doing well on different marketplaces.

Social Shopping Websites

There are different social shopping websites or online marketplaces that are curated by not just users but even the tastemakers. They are quite helpful since they list the products that appeal to online shoppers. It will also help you gain insight into the kind of products that are trending and are popular before they become mainstream. These websites will save you time and you don't have to go through the thousands of product lists on your supplier's websites or other platforms like eBay or Amazon. Instead they offer a curated list of items based on current trends in the market. A couple of places that you can visit to gather this information are wanelo.co/stores, fancy.com/shop, wish.com, and etsy.com.

e-Commerce Stores

When you are thinking about the different products that you can dropship, it helps to learn from those dropshippers who are doing well in the field. You can look at the different products that the successful e-commerce stores are selling. Make a note of their listings, the photography, and the sales copy they use. All this can act as inspiration and help you come up with product ideas of your own. Going through the websites of your competitors will also help you visualize how your online store will look.

Retail Price

The price at which you can sell the product for is known as retail price. Ideally, as a dropshipper, you must opt for products that can be retailed for anywhere between $15 and $200. It might sound like quite a margin between these two numbers, but it is considered something of a sweet spot if you are interested in dropshipping. There are multiple reasons why the best dropshipping products retail for this price range and they include the following:

If you are selling a product that is perceived as being affordable, then it is quite likely that you will be able to sell high volumes of such a product. If you can sell high volumes of a product, then it increases the chances of obtaining customer feedback. Customer feedback is critical when you are building your credibility as a dropshipper. If you sell the products for less than $15, then it will significantly lower your profit margins and you will need to sell a lot of stock. On the other hand, if the product retails for over $200, then it is not considered to be affordable and it can be quite difficult to sell. Also, if you sell products for more than $200, then when you need to make any refunds, it can really burn a hole in your pocket.

So, does that mean that you can never sell over

$200 per product? Well, the only time you can go higher than $150 is when you are able to sell the products with a minimum advertised price or a minimum retail price (MRP). If a product has an MRP, it means that you cannot sell the product for a price that's less than the MRP set by the manufacturer. For instance, Apple has a strict MRP policy on their products and no retailer can offer a better deal on iPhones than any of its competitors in the market. Opting for MRP products is a good idea because it prevents dropshippers from competing on the price and, instead, they need to focus on the value addition and the benefits they can offer customers. If you are just getting started with dropshipping, then it is a good idea to stick to this price limit.

Recommended Margin

The product that you want to dropship needs to offer a profit margin of at least 20-40%. The profit margin of a dropshipper is usually higher since sellers have the option to markup their retail price by 100% or even more. If you are dropshipping a product that retails for $200, then you can have a profit margin of up to 30% on such a product and you will be left with a profit of about $60 per order. If you decide to sell a product that retails for $20, then you must increase your profit margin on such a product. Remember that while you are setting your margin on the product you want to dropship, there are a couple of things that you need to take into account like packaging costs, shipping charges, marketing costs, and any other expenses that you might incur while making a sale. Therefore, it is always a good idea to opt for a product that offers a high-profit margin.

Weight and Size

Ideally, the best products for dropshipping are those that can easily fit into a shoebox. Anything larger than that and it will increase your shipping costs. You need to be mindful of the weight and size of the product if you want to be a successful dropshipper. The profit margin of your product will decrease considerably if you have a very high shipping cost. Most dropshippers tend to use ePacket as their shipping partner. ePacket is a shipping service that allows the users to quickly ship products from China or Hong Kong to the United States and over 30 other countries. If you want to use a shipping service like ePacket, you must be mindful of the size and the weight of the products. ePacket has a minimum and a maximum weight requirement for the products they ship. If you want to take up dropshipping, then you must look for products that are small, weigh less, and are easy to ship.

Moving Parts

An ideal product for dropshipping is one in which little can go wrong. You must avoid products that are fragile or fiddly, since they can easily break while being shipped and it will result in a lot of negative feedback from customers. Electrical gadgets fall into this category, especially if you are working with an unfamiliar supplier. It is a good idea to stick to products that are sturdy and can sustain the international shipping process.

Potential Repeat Business

One criterion that a lot of new dropshippers forget is that a great product means repeat business. It means that if the product is something that the customer likes, then it is quite likely that such a customer will be potentially a repeat buyer. A new concept that has become quite popular these days is the idea of subscription services. There are businesses that offer everything from luxury chocolates to feminine hygiene products that are delivered monthly to subscribers. This gives the seller a predictable monthly business. The ideal categories for this sort of business model are the products that fall into the category of health and beauty products that a person needs to purchase every time they run out. If you can successfully convert a customer, then the chances of repeat business increase, so try to check for products that you can use for a subscription service.

Supplier

Selecting the product is as important as selecting the right supplier for your dropshipping business. Without a good supplier, you cannot fulfill your orders on time and it will not help you with your business. As a dropshipper, you will potentially rely on the supplier to manufacture the product, maintain sufficient inventory, and ship it to the customer in a timely fashion. You will learn more about selecting a supplier in the coming chapters.

Low Turnover

The product that you want to dropship must be something that will stay in production constantly. If you want to dropship a product, then you will need to invest in good quality photographs and sales copy for the product listings. If you opt for a product that will stay in production at any given time, then you can make your investment in photography and the likes last you longer. Products with a high turnover (the products that get discontinued quickly or change every couple of months) are not a good option since you will need to constantly spend money to upgrade and revamp the website and your product list.

Trials

This is an exciting step while selecting a product. If you have a dropshipping idea that made it through the previous steps and it seems like a good idea, then you need to think about whether the product will work or not. A product might look great on paper, but it needs to do well in real life as well, so the best way to test a product is to order it for a trial. It helps to test the quality of the product and the efficiency of the supplier as well.

Mistakes to Avoid

Mistakes are inevitable, and they are a part of the learning process. It is okay to make mistakes, but it will be wonderful if you can learn from the mistakes of others. In this section you will learn about the common mistakes that dropshippers make while choosing products. If you can avoid these mistakes, you will increase the profitability of your business.

You must never opt for a branded or designer product. A lot of people get tempted by big brand and designer products and they think that they can earn a lot of money by dropshipping such products. Big brands are always well known and are quite expensive and always in demand. The profit margins on such products are quite low and this makes it a very bad option for dropshippers. Unless you think you have the buying power of a huge retail store, then you must stay away from big brand products. The best products for dropshippers are generic products or private label products.

It might seem tempting to sell imitation or knockoff products since they are also always in demand, but it is a bad idea to do this. You must steer clear of all counterfeit products if you want to avoid any legal troubles and don't want to jeopardize your dropshipping business. Stay away from suppliers of those branded goods who are selling at prices that sound too good to be true.

Another common mistake that a lot of newbie dropshippers make is that they opt for highly competitive products. You might think that you have found a great product for your business since it is in demand. You must remember that others might have also thought the same and must be selling the same product. Lots of other dropshippers might be selling such products on other websites. If it is a hot product, then it must also be all over social media and you might think of it as a winning strategy. It is a bad idea to sell those products that are highly competitive. A good amount of competition in the niche you select does show that the product you opted for is successful, but it also means that you will need to compete with all those sellers who are selling the same product.

Chapter 4: How to Create your Dropshipping Website

Build Dropshipping Website with Shopify

In this section, you will learn about building a professional dropshipping website with Shopify. There are ten simple steps discussed in this section and if you follow them you will have a fully functional dropshipping website within no time. Building a dropshipping website will not cost you more than $70 and will take you up to a day.

Step One: Register

The first thing to do is register yourself with Shopify. You can use the 14-day free trial option to get a feel of Shopify. You need to enter the store name. If the store name that you want is not available, then Shopify will not let you proceed. Once you enter your name and other contact details, it will prompt you to enter details about the stage your business is in at present. If you go to the administrator page, you will find the option of "Add Online Store." Click on this option. The dropshipping business will make sales only through the online website, so you need to select this option.

Step Two: Website Domain

You need to buy your web domain. If you don't, then you run the risk of someone else buying the domain that you want. What will happen if you don't buy a domain? It doesn't mean that your business will not be functional, but the URL will look less professional. For instance, if you are on Shopify to dropship standing desks, then the URL of the store (if you don't purchase the domain) might look like "yourStandingDesk.myshopify.com." it certainly doesn't look professional does it? If your URL doesn't look professional, then the customers or suppliers might be under the impression that you aren't a legitimate business.

If you want to buy a domain name, you need to click on the "online store" option and select the "Domains" option. From there you need to click on "Buy new Domain" to purchase a domain name. For instance, if you want to purchase the domain name www.yourstandingdesk.com then you will have to search for the same in the search tab and then check the availability of the domain name. Shopify will let you know whether the domain name you want is available or not. If the domain name is available, then you need to enter the billing details to purchase it.

As soon as you purchase the domain name, Shopify will redirect you to a page asking if you want to direct all the web traffic to the new domain. Since your answer is yes, you need to select the domain name and click save. As soon as you purchase the domain name, Shopify will send you an email alerting you about the domain you just purchased. Ensure that you verify this purchase. If you don't, then your domain will be suspended. It might seem like a simple step, but if you don't do this, then you cannot use your domain name.

Step Three: Email Forwarding

After you purchase and verify your domain name, you need to set up an email forwarding address for your store. To do this, you need to go to the menu and select the "Online Store" option and click on "Domains." You will see a "manage domains" tab and click on it. Shopify will redirect you to a page that says, "Email Forwarding."

What does email forwarding mean? It means that if a customer or supplier emails you on your Shopify website, it will forward that email to another address of your choosing. Shopify will automatically set up two email forwarding addresses and they are info@ your domain name or sales@ your domain name. You need to remember that Shopify allows visitors to reach your account with your domain name in it, but since it doesn't host the email for you, the reply to all the emails will come from the email account that the email was forwarded to.

Step Four: Shopify Theme

Shopify helps you build good looking desktop and mobile sites. The platform is quite easy to use and the theme you select is quite important. The theme of the store will lend the store a structure and will make it seem legitimate. To select the theme, you need to visit the "online store" menu and opt for the "Themes" option. You will find the option "visit theme store" and click on it. It will open another tab with the Shopify's theme store. Shopify offers various paid-for and free themes. You can search for themes according to their price, popularity, or other specific filters. If you find a theme that appeals to you, click on the "view demo" option to see how the theme will look on your page. Once you find a theme that you like, click on "Install Theme." You will be prompted if you want to publish the theme as your shop's theme or install it as an unpublished theme. If you select the unpublished theme option, it will not be visible on your online store.

You can customize the theme to suit your store's needs to attract customers.

Step Five: Important Pages

There are a couple of pages that are preloaded with the theme. Shopify doesn't know all your requirements, so you need to include certain "must have" pages to the store. The important pages for your dropshipping business website include the homepage, about us page, product page, shipping and returns page, and a contact us page.

Step Six: Add Products

This is when things will get quite exciting for your store. Up until now you were concentering on setting up the store. Now, you can add products to your store. Go to the "online store" option and click on the "products" tab. Once you do this, you can click on the "add product" tab to start adding products. When you click on this option, Shopify will direct you to a page where you can start adding details about your first product.

You can obtain the information that you decide to use along with the pictures from your supplier's website. Most suppliers tend to have a lot of information about their products listed like the description, specifications, photos, and maybe some other sales materials. Suppliers try to provide their partners with all the information that they will need to build their brands. The first thing that you need to do is enter the name of the product then write its description along with any specifications. Then you need to click on the "organization" option. There are three ways in which you can organize your product list.

The first one is product type. It helps you group different types of products based on the kind of products you want to sell.

The second one is according to the vendor. It allows you to group products according to the vendor you obtain them from.

The third option is according to collections. You can create a group of specially curated products with this option.

Apart from this, you can also add tags that will make it easy to search for your products.

By doing this, you make it quite simple for customers to find your products. After you organize the products, you need to upload pictures and set the price.

Step Seven: Theme Customization

When you were customizing your theme initially, you had no content on the site. Now that you have the necessary content along with the must-have pages, you can customize the theme of the Shopify store. You can now add links to your other social media accounts to make it easier for customers to reach you.

Step Eight: Customer Review App

Shopify has a good app store. There are several

add-ons and plug-ins that you will find on this store. You can use these to improve the quality of your Shopify store. There are several free and paid-for apps that you can download. One thing that you must add is the Customer Review app. This app doesn't cost you anything and, once you install this on your site, customers can leave their reviews on it. If you want to build your online presence and your credibility as a dropshipper, then you will need customer reviews. The best way to do this is to add the customer review app.

Step Nine: Shopify Plan

You need to pick a Shopify plan for your store. The 14-day free trial option is great to familiarize yourself with the website, but now that you are ready to jump into the game, you need to select a plan that suits your needs. When you are selecting a plan for your Shopify store, there are a couple of things that you must keep in mind. You need to remember that contracts are on a month-to-month basis, unless you sign up for the biennial or annual plan. If you subscribe for the annual or biennial plan, then it entitles to you a certain discount. You have the option of canceling the plan whenever you want to. Apart from this, you can also upgrade or downgrade the plan whenever you like.

The different plans that Shopify offers are:

The Starter plan costs about $14 per month and you cannot list more than 25 products under this option. Also, it doesn't entitle you to any phone support from Shopify.

The Basic plan costs $29 per month and allows you to list unlimited products. It also entitles you to sell on social media and offers 24/7-customer support service.

The Professional plan will cost you $79 per month. It offers cart recovery options, better reporting, slightly lower credit card processing rate, and also offers the Basic plus gift cards.

The Unlimited plan will cost you $179 per month and offers everything that the Professional plan offers along with precise reporting. Also, the credit card processing fees are even lower if you opt for this plan.

Since you are just getting started with dropshipping, it is a good idea to start with the Basic plan.

Step Ten: Check Settings

The last step is to check all your Shopify settings once again. Check all the information that you added in each section. Once you are happy with all the information you have added, you can go ahead and launch your website on Shopify.

Creating your Dropshipping Website with Selz

Now that you know what dropshipping is about, the next step is to create your dropshipping website. Do you want to create an online store, but don't want to spend thousands of your hard-earned dollars to build an e-commerce website? If yes, then go through the simple steps given in this section to build your dropshipping website.

Select a Domain Name

The first thing that you need to do is select a domain for your dropshipping website. Do you need a custom domain for your e-commerce site? Yes, you absolutely do! When you register with Selz (it's absolutely free by the way) you will be given a sub-domain along the lines of "mysite.selz.com." This might serve the purpose for your e-commerce site, but, if you want to sell a variety of products or develop a brand, then you will need a custom domain name. A custom domain address or name gives you a recognizable brand that belongs solely to you. It gives you a professional email address that's linked to your domain so that people can contact you. It also helps with SEO strategies. It is quite easy to create a custom domain name on Selz and all it takes are a couple of clicks. If you have a domain name, then you can quickly configure the settings on Selz. If you don't have one and you want one, then you can purchase it quickly from the Selz dashboard.

Select the Right Platform

This is quite easy. You will want an e-commerce platform that offers flexibility and is easy to use. Most business owners don't like the idea of being bothered with coding their website. Either that or they don't know how to code. As a dropshipper, you are a business owner and you will need a platform that you can easily integrate with your existing site. If you don't have a website yet, then you will need a platform that allows you to build your site from scratch. It is helpful to have a platform that allows you to do this easily. Selz will help you design a professional and stylish website and it is quite affordable. Also, you have the option to customize your website.

Design

The next step is to design your online store. There are various easy-to-use and beautiful themes available with the option of customization. You can view the demo or the previews of different themes to select one that meets your needs and helps you showcase your products in the best possible manner. You also have the option of adding pages, products, blog posts, videos, text, and much more to your online store. Doing this will pique a customer's curiosity and will also make them feel comfortable about making a purchase. You need to include an "About Us" page along with a "Contact Us" page while designing your store. It provides your customers with an option to contact you easily.

Payments

There are two aspects of payment that you need to consider. The first aspect is about how the customers can pay you and the second one is about how you can transfer those funds to your bank account. There are multiple payment options acceptable on Selz, so go through them to choose the ones that best suit your needs.

Add Products

You need to add products to your e-commerce

site. An e-commerce website without any products on display is like a retail store without any items on display. You need to select the products, then add their description, insert the necessary images, set their price, create a preview of the items, and select the delivery options.

Test the Checkout

For any e-commerce business, the shopping cart being abandoned is a major problem. You need to make sure that this doesn't happen. To prevent it, you must ensure that the checkout section of the website is not just enabled and optimized for desktops, but for mobile and tablet users as well. Include the option of allowing customers to purchase multiple items at once. You can also send a cart abandonment email to the customer if they leave their cart at checkout and don't complete their purchase. Another option that you have to reduce the instances of cart abandonment is to offer free shipping whenever possible.

Once you set up your online store, you must start

marketing your store if you want to earn a profit. You will learn about the different marketing techniques that you can use in the coming chapters.

You can use either of the methods to create your dropshipping website. Your dropshipping website is your online storefront. So, you need to make sure that it not only looks appealing, but also attracts customers to make a purchase. Setting up your website will enable you to start selling. If you want to earn the financial stability that you always dreamt of, then you need to boost your sales and a good dropshipping website will help you achieve this objective.

Chapter 5: Find the Best Suppliers

Finding the right supplier is quintessential for your success as a dropshipper. If you find a good supplier, your business will not only be more credible and popular, but it will also help you earn better profits. Keep the simple tips discussed in this chapter in mind while selecting a supplier for your business. The right supplier can help you earn more than 100k in a month from your dropshipping store.

Find a Top-Tier Supplier

Dropshipping has become a popular business model these days. It is quite easy to start your own dropshipping store. If you want your dropshipping store to be successful, then the most important aspect is to find the right supplier. You might have spent a lot of time building your website, selecting the products, and promoting it as well. All your efforts will amount to nothing if you don't find a credible supplier. A bad supplier can damage your credibility and hard work quite easily. Finding an online supplier is not an easy task and it does take a while to find the best supplier. Well, don't worry about all this. The information given in this section will help you find the best suppliers for your dropshipping business.

So, when must you start looking for a supplier? There are two instances when you will look for a supplier. The first one is when you are looking for a product as well as a supplier and the second instance is when you select a product and are looking for a supplier of that product. Let us look at both these scenarios.

You might know someone who has an e-commerce store that you like or might want to get started with dropshipping. To start your dropshipping business, you will not only need a product that you want to dropship but will also need a supplier. Since you are just starting out, you can simultaneously search for a supplier as well as a product. Take a look at different offline businesses that haven't stepped into the online world. Consider if what they are offering can be sold online or not and you can make a list of all the ideas you get. When you find a good idea, you must ask the business if they want to sell their products online for a commission. If the business that you want to approach has no online presence, then the term dropshipping will not be relevant to them, so you will need to explain your business idea to them and ask them for their opinions or interest. Try to find a supplier who isn't too far away from you. Your supplier is a partner in your business model, so it is always better to find someone who is located nearby.

If you already have a specific product in mind, then you will need to look for a supplier. Dropshipping is a good idea if you want a business model with less risk and no inventory. Now, you need to find suppliers who can sell their product to you.

As a dropshipper, you will be fully dependent on your supplier to fulfill all your orders. There are some suppliers who are not only reliable but always have good stock in hand so that they can ship the products promptly. If you find a supplier who does all this, then such a supplier is a top-tier supplier. On the other hand, a not-so-good supplier will do the exact opposite of all that's desirable and it will increase your business costs.

Once you have identified your niche and your competition, you need to identify suppliers. Don't worry about contacting suppliers as of now, but you need to work on impressing your prospects. To do this, you need to research your niche and take a look at the suppliers your competitors use. Instead of approaching unproven suppliers, it is a good idea to obtain the information that you gather by researching your niche. It is quite easy to identify the products and the brands that are performing well for your competitors. The products that are doing well are usually listed front and center on the official business website to increase their visibility to the customers. The products can also be listed under the most popular products or categories pages as well.

Now, you need to get working and make a list of all the different brands, the product names, and the stock keeping unit numbers related to your niche. You must repeat this step for all your competitors. Once you do this, you will be left with not just a list of products that are doing well, but also the information about different suppliers that your competitors are using.

You might be wondering if there was a simpler way to make a list of the top-tier sellers in your chosen niche. The suppliers that you are looking for don't necessarily have a good marketing strategy in place, so you will need to do the necessary legwork to locate them, so if you want to dropship standing desks and you search for something along the lines of "standing desk dropshipping suppliers" it is highly unlikely that you will find a reliable dropshipping supplier. In fact, the Google search might display supplier aggregators instead.

Aggregators know that dropshippers find it difficult to find suppliers, so they usually sell the access to the list of suppliers that they compile. For a new dropshipper, this might look like a viable option. After all, you merely need to pay a fee to obtain a list of suppliers. Sounds perfect, doesn't it? Well, it isn't a good idea. Aggregators tend to attract a lot of dropshippers who are looking for shortcuts and a top-tier seller will not want to associate themselves with someone who is looking for shortcuts. The top-tier sellers might also not like the idea of screening through the list of dropshippers to find someone who means serious business, so an aggregator might help you connect with a supplier, but it is quite likely that the supplier is not necessarily a top-tier supplier. A couple of popular aggregators that you can use are Worldwide Brands, DOBA, and DropshipDirect. While you are looking at the websites of your competitors, you can make a list of the things that you like and dislike about their websites along with a list of their suppliers. Once you make a list of all potential suppliers, the next step is to verify the suppliers. To do this, there are two things that you must consider: the enforcement of their MAP policies and if they are no pay-to-play or not.

The MAP policies or the Minimum Advertised Price policies are the set of rules that a supplier has in place to protect their business value as well as that of their partners. It is the lowest price at which a retailer can sell the supplier's products. You must always work with a supplier who enforces their MAP policies. The enforceability of these policies is important, because without it there will be a price war amongst dropshippers. A price war is nothing but a race to the bottom. As a dropshipper, your profit margin will decrease along with the brand value of your supplier. A top-tier will be particular about the strict enforcement of their MAP policies.

To check whether a supplier enforces their MAP policies or not, you need to simply search for their product on Google Shopping. You will be able to see multiple listings for a specific product. You are trying to check the lowest common price for a product. For instance, if the lowest listing for a product is $34 and no retailer seems to be listing it for anything below that figure, then it means that the supplier enforces their MAP policies. For a dropshipper, the MAP also represents the lowest profit margin that's available on a product. If the margin is lean, then you need to look for some other product with a better margin.

While searching for suppliers, if you come across any suppliers who charge an annual or monthly fee to sell their products, then such a supplier is not a top-tier supplier. It indicates that the supplier is more interested in making money than building their brand. A top-tier supplier usually values a dropshipping store since it provides a business opportunity for the supplier to introduce their products to a greater audience. A simple email can help you find whether the supplier has a pay-to-play policy or not. Most suppliers will provide their contact information for this purpose. Here are a couple of other things that you need to keep in mind while selecting a supplier.

The supplier that you opt for must be a professional. Dropshipping requires a professional relationship and there are various agreements that need to be upheld. Don't entrust the credibility of your business in the hands of the first person that makes an offer.

A trait of professionalism is punctuality. You need a supplier who not only understands the need for punctuality in business but is punctual as well. If the supplier is not punctual with the delivery of orders, then it is the credibility of your business that will be hurt.

Proximity is a good factor to consider. It is not necessarily compulsory, but it is always better to have a supplier in close proximity. Getting to know your supplier will do your business a lot of good.

If the supplier that you are interested in is also the supplier for several other dropshipping businesses in your niche, then it can be a tough job to make your business stand out from that of your competitors.

Before you finalize a supplier, make sure that you have a business contract in place that dictates the terms of service and payment.

If you find a supplier who meets all these criteria, then you have found yourself a good supplier.

Negotiate with a Supplier

In this section, you will learn about the different practices that you can adopt while negotiating with a potential supplier for your dropshipping business.

Your Business

The first thing that you need to keep in mind is your dropshipping business. There are two possible scenarios in this situation: you have an established dropshipping business or you are starting from scratch.

If you have an established dropshipping business, then you are certainly negotiating from a position of power. If you have a project that's working and has potential buyers, then it certainly gives you some authority while negotiating. For instance, let us assume that you are an e-commerce business that sells backpacks and have started to review different models and brands in this niche. Once your website gained about 100 visitors a day, you decided to move onto affiliate marketing. After this, you started looking for a supplier to change your business model from affiliate marketing to dropshipping. This will be easy to negotiate since you have a website that's well-positioned and you can use these analytics while looking for a supplier. If you have a well-positioned website with good traffic, then it gives you an advantage. In fact, it is a win-win situation for both the parties that are involved. The dropshipper will gain access to new clients and you can increase your income.

Now, let us consider a scenario where you are trying to negotiate with nothing to show for your business. This is the most likely scenario for anyone who is just getting started with dropshipping. You can promise great sales, but you don't have concrete proof of it. The dropshipping supplier will need to take your word for it. Think about it from the perspective of the supplier. It is nearly impossible to assure any future sales, so why must the supplier work with you? A common mistake that a lot of newcomers make is that they try to negotiate great commissions without any traffic to their website. If that's the case, then try to be humble and don't pretend to be something that you aren't and certainly don't make any promises that you cannot withhold.

Legal

The suppliers will certainly hesitate to dropship their products if you aren't a registered business. If you don't register your online store (or register yourself as a freelancer), then it will be quite impossible to find you. Is there a specific kind of contract that you need to sign with your supplier? There are a couple of things that you must include in your contract. You need to include different clauses regarding communication, commission, payment, shipping, compensations, and responsibilities of both the parties.

When it comes to communication, please include the form of communication that you plan to use. How will you inform the supplier about the order? How long can the supplier take to confirm the receipt of the order? Think about all this carefully and make a provision for the same in your dropshipping contract.

Commission is an important part of a dropshipping business. What is the percentage that you expect from every sale? You need to ask for a commission of at least 15% and nothing less than 25-30% if the products are low-priced. It isn't just the commission that you need to agree on, but the method of payment and the payment period, so what is the method of payment you want to use and by when do you want to receive the payment? Usually, it is a good practice to pay the supplier after you make a sale. Also, don't pay the supplier before the period of return expires. For instance, think of a situation where you have paid the supplier and then the client returns the product. All this is nothing but hassle for you and you need to strive to avoid it. If you are working with foreign suppliers, then take into account the exchange rates while deciding the payment method and commission.

The contract with your supplier needs to include clauses regarding returns and guarantees. The contract needs to specify what will happen when the customer returns an order, who will bear the expenses of the return and who needs to take care of any replacement.

When you are dropshipping products, you need to make sure that the products are shipped to the customer within a specific period in a specific condition. Dropshipper supplier needs to comply with these dates and ship it in a manner you both agreed on. Also, include a clause for compensations. In case of any non-compliance with any of the terms of the contract, there needs to be a compensation that needs to be paid. Signing the contract is quintessential and it makes the agreement legally binding for both parties.

Beware of who you talk to

Merely because a supplier wants to work with you doesn't make such a supplier a good fit. There are a lot of suppliers out there who will try to deceive you to earn a quick buck, so you must be careful about who you talk to. There is an easy way to spot such people. If the supplier asks for a commission or a fee for dropshipping, then steer clear of such people.

Supplier Directories

There are several directories that include various companies located all over the globe that provide goods to be dropshipped to different countries. Regardless of the country that you want to establish your dropshipping business in, you will find a directory that you can use. Use these directories to verify the credibility of the dropshipper, but don't trust the information given on them blindly and do the necessary homework to vet the suppliers. You will need to pay a small fee to access such a directory. Two of the most commonly used online directories are WholesaleCentral and SaleHoo.

Use Google

There will be plenty of suppliers who aren't registered on the directories, so what do you do in such a case? Well, the answer is simple. You can look for them on Google. Search for the specific product you want to sell and all the suppliers who sell such products. You will need to spend some time doing all the research because it is likely that the suppliers you are looking for don't rank first in SEO results. Most wholesalers don't make any marketing or advertising efforts, so don't be surprised if you find your supplier on the 15th page of the search results instead of the first one.

Change Your Supplier

If you are working with a specific supplier and you think that things aren't going as they are supposed to, then don't be afraid to find another supplier. You must remember that you are in it for the business and if a supplier does your business no good, then why must you retain such a supplier? Don't be afraid to change your supplier if things don't work out well for you.

Chapter 6: Affiliate Marketing

Steps to Find a Product to Promote

The success of an affiliate marketer depends on the products that they choose to promote. At first, it might seem simple to find a product to promote. Once you sign up with ClickBank, you will realize that there are tens of thousands of products and thousands of vendors to choose from. Well, you might choose a product and create a HopLink that you add to your website and think your work is all done; however, after a couple of weeks, you might start to wonder why you haven't been able to make any sales. A sneaking suspicion might creep in about whether you made the right choice by selecting the product you did or not. The amount of selection available on ClickBank can be quite overwhelming for anyone, so how do you select a product that will sell well? What about the existing competition and what do all these numbers mean to you? There is no fixed formula that you can follow while selecting a product to promote. Here are a couple of different tips that will help you make the right choice.

Niche

The first thing that you need to do is think about the market that you want to work in. While selecting the market you want to take up affiliate marketing in, then select something that interests you. It is always a good idea to select a niche that's related to your interests. You can select a niche that's related to your hobbies, passions, skills, or it can even be something that you have a lot of experience in. Being knowledgeable about the niche that you select will certainly come in handy when you are creating your marketing campaigns, so go through ClickBank's massive marketplace and create a list of all the niches that interest you and you will want to promote. It is not just about selecting a niche; you must also make sure that the niche you selected is a profitable one.

Understand your audience

For instance, you added "playing guitar" to the list that you made in the previous step while looking for niches. If you want to take this idea further, then it is important that you understand two things - who are present in the niche and what are they buying at present? The simplest way in which you can gain some insight into the minds of your customers is by going through all those forums related to your niche. This will help you understand the needs, wants, and the problems of your potential buyers. For instance, if you want to concentrate on the guitar market, then some people might be looking for guitar sheet music and they might not be interested in buying anything from you. Then there will be some people who might want to learn to play guitar quickly for some reason or other and these are the ones who are likely to purchase something that will help them achieve their objective. Going through different guitar forums will help you understand things, like the guitars that most people play, and it will help you select the best products to promote.

Best-Sellers

By now, you know about your market and what the audience is looking for. It is time to go back to ClickBank and look for some good products that will meet the needs of your audience. "Gravity" is a metric that ClickBank uses to denote how well a product is selling. It is based on the number of sales that were made and the recency of the sales.

If a product has gravity of over 100, then it is said to be quite high and it indicates that there is a lot of competition that exists in the niche. Don't let this discourage you. Competition implies that there is plenty of demand for the product in a niche. Don't let gravity be the only metric that you take into consideration while selecting a product. At times, a product might have low gravity merely because it hasn't been discovered yet. Gravity is a helpful indicator regarding the demand for a product, but you must not reject a high-quality product because it has low gravity.

Multiple Products

You must try to find a niche that has several related products that are being sold on ClickBank. The reason why you must do this is even if there is only one profitable product in a niche and it has a high demand, then you will have a tough time competing with all the well-established and existing sellers in the niche. If you find a niche with multiple products, then you can create a review page and increase the likelihood of making a sale. For instance, if you are selling a product "learn to play guitar" and you include a couple of other "learn guitar" products on a page, then the visitor will feel like he or she has made it through the evaluation phase and now wants to purchase something.

High Commission

If you want to make it big in the field of affiliate

marketing, then you need to promote those products that offer a high commission. The commission payable to you per sale needs to be $18 or higher, if you want to get rich! You need to keep in mind that even if the commission seems quite significant, you need to make allowances for your marketing and advertising expenses and your time spent on affiliate marketing; however, if you find a product with a high dollar value, then even a commission of a lower percentage will do you good.

Vendor's Pitch

You need to look at the different product's sales pages since you will be relying on this page to convert your HopLinks into a steady income. Does the page look convincing? Do you think it addresses the concerns present in the market? Is the pitch persuasive and convincing? If you have to, will you buy from such a page?

Selecting the right product to promote is the first step to becoming a successful affiliate marketer.

If you get this step right, the chances of your success increase rather drastically.

Promote Affiliate Products to Your Email List

Encouraging and motivating people to purchase the products you are promoting is an important skill for an affiliate. This skill is quite important if you want to become a successful affiliate marketer. If you want to become a successful affiliate marketer, then you must be able to drive traffic to your business website, maintain a subscriber list, and follow up with them on a regular basis. Email marketing is quite helpful if you want to build and maintain customer relationships. The one thing that you must understand about affiliate marketing is that it works on the subtle power of suggestion and isn't about hard selling. As an affiliate marketer, you need to gently coax people and encourage them to buy the products that you are advertising. If you turn to any hard-selling tactics, then it will act as a turn-off. Remember the old saying "people hate to be sold but love to buy"? Bear this in mind when you are thinking about affiliate marketing.

Social media marketing is certainly all the rage these days and sending out emails is one of the best promotional tools that you can use to create awareness and for promotion in affiliate marketing. Email marketing is quite simple. You need to build an email list and then you need to keep sending interesting and engaging content to the subscribers on your list to maintain a good customer relationship with them.

As an affiliate marketer, you need to make sure that the emails you are sending seem more conversational and not business like. When you are selling to your email list, please make sure that you use plain text and don't bombard the reader with various glaring images. Affiliate marketers usually get carried away with new tactics that can attract the attention of the reader but don't usually lead to conversions.

When you are selling to your email list, you need

to make sure you are clearly explaining all the benefits of the products you are promoting without sounding like you are hard selling.

The emails you send need to be optimized for mobile usage. The usage of mobile devices has grown in leaps and bounds and relying on any technology that does not support these devices is a sure shot way to lose out on plenty of business opportunities.

Your sales pitch needs to short, and you must avoid adding repetitive content. Also, try to personalize your emails to build a better relationship with the subscriber.

You can always include affiliate links in the emails you send, but don't go overboard and don't include multiple links. A link or two is fine, but don't include more links than that.

At times, it might seem difficult to sell a product or even market a service when you cannot reach your target audience. At times, you will need different means to sell the products or even earn some extra income. In such situations, affiliate marketing is a good idea. In affiliate marketing, the seller sells the products with the help of the promotional services of an affiliate. The affiliate helps promote and market the product to potential customers. It helps the vendor make a sale and in turn, the vendor will pay the affiliate a commission for making this possible. Affiliate marketing is quite popular these days and it can be something as simple as reviewing a product on social media. In this section, you will learn about the different things that you need to keep in mind while selecting an affiliate program and earning money as an affiliate.

Other Tips

Ads and Reviews

If you want to promote your affiliate products, you can use classified sites. There are different classified sites that you can use like craigslist and eBay that you can use to search for any product that you want. You can use the same platform to promote your affiliate products as well. While you are posting your affiliate links on such sites, you can even write ads and reviews for the products you want to promote.

Pay Per Click (PPC)

This method is not usually the best method to promote affiliate products. By opting for this method, you need to create several pay-per-click (PPC) campaigns using different search engines like Google, Yahoo, Bing and so on. Once you create such a campaign, you need to promote the merchant website by using the affiliate link. This method of promotion is anything but straightforward. Instead of directly using PPC to promote your affiliate products, you will be directing all the traffic to your merchant's website.

There are two things that you need to keep in mind before you opt for this method. There is a chance that the merchant website might not even accept the affiliate link. You will be competing with other advertisers for the space that's available. If your ad isn't attractive or well-written, then you will find yourself in a world of trouble. The other thing that you need to keep in mind is that you have absolutely no control over the quality of the merchant's website. If the website lacks good content or has poor content, then you will end up spending more money than that's necessary.

Blogs and Forums

The first thing that you need to do is select a product that you like and you want to promote. Once you do this, you need to start advertising about the product on different forums and blogs. So, how can you direct the users towards the affiliate link that you post? The answer is quite simple- use the affiliate link as the signature. If you can make yourself an active member on the forum and if you have a good number of followers, then it will work well for you. A word of caution- you need to be careful about the kind of blogs or forums that you decide to use to market your affiliate products. You need to target such platforms that are complimentary to your product or are similar to what you are promoting. For instance, if you want to market a product related to fashion, then opting for a blog that's related to car décor will not make any sense.

Guidelines

If you want to make a good impression on a public platform, then you need to be mindful of the content that you post. You must make sure that the content that you are posting is not merely entertaining but is helpful as well. Follow the guidelines of the platform and don't post anything that is in violation of the rules and regulations of your chosen platform. If you post any unsuitable content or content that violates the terms of service of a given platform, then your content can be banned from such a site and your account can be blocked as well.

A simple Google search for "affiliate marketing programs" will display thousands of results.

Some of these platforms might ask you to pay a fee to join their affiliate marketing program. Usually they use fancy downloadable applications along with "well-thought out" payment plans. Apart from all this, they also usually hike their fee by mentioning special discounts and offers to lure unsuspecting users, so what can you do if you come across such a platform? You are not supposed to do anything, you must merely move onto the next option.

When you are selecting an affiliate program, let your instinct guide you and don't give in to the temptation of any of these jazzy schemes you come across. You must remember that the affiliate business will not pay you a commission until they make a sale and they need your help to accomplish this. You are helping them, aren't you? So, does it make any sense to pay the business to let you help them? That sounds obnoxious, doesn't it? At times it might feel like you have found the perfect platform, especially when they promise a lot of things. Please don't fall into this trap and never give out your credit card details. If the site seems spurious, move onto the next site and don't linger there. As a general rule of thumb, it is wise to stay away from websites that promise the world to you, provided you pay a fee!

The affiliates you want to promote need to add some value to your site along with your visitors and must complement you. If you want to increase your website traffic and want to increase the business of the affiliate, then you need to look for the best affiliates available. You must ensure that you do a little research before you decide on an affiliate. You can select any affiliate that you want to work with. Check a couple of websites that other bloggers host. Once you find what you are looking for, you can contact them and show them the blog or the website you maintain. Make a list of the businesses that you want to pair up with and you can work from there. It is important that you believe in the business before you decide to become an affiliate for them.

Once you are happy and confident about the

business that you choose, and you want to provide your loyal customers with good service, you need to talk about the terms and conditions. After all, you must be fully aware of their terms and conditions before you decide to associate yourself with a specific business. You must understand how their affiliate program works. Find the necessary details about their payment policy and the modes of payment. Will you be paid per sale or will you be given a commission for generating leads? If you are negotiating these terms, then always opt for commission based on any leads you generate.

Once you are aware of their payment mechanism, you must find out about the frequency of payments. Commission rates tend to differ from one business to another, so make sure that the commission you are being paid is worth all the effort that you put in. Money is an important variable, but that's not the only thing that matters. You will be promoting a product or service, so you need to make sure that what you are promoting lives up to what the business believes. Discuss your rights and terms of the termination clause. Make an official record of all this and store it. Making a note of all this is important if you don't want to run into any legal troubles later.

Earn from Affiliate Marketing

Becoming an affiliate marketer is a great way to earn passive income. To build a passive income stream, you will need to dedicate the necessary time and effort. You cannot expect your business to be successful overnight and you need to stay patient. Here are a couple of things that you can do to increase your income from affiliate marketing.

Build your Website Traffic

An important thing for affiliate marketing is the interest of people in clicking on different links to the products that catch their attention. Who are all these "people?" These people are all those readers who visit your blog or your website. If you want to lure these people, then you need to make your blog as interesting as possible. You can go out of your way and decorate the website or blog as much as you want. While doing this, make sure that the theme of the website is in sync with the content that you post. You must have a good readership or audience base; if you don't, then who will you market to? Not just that, but why will a business pay you if you don't have an audience to market to? The greater your reach, the higher your chances of increasing your reach. The greater your reach the higher the chances of making a sale for the business you are an affiliate for.

A Good Product or Service Will Do

A lot of newbies make the mistake of flooding their sites with different products thinking that people will want to buy more if they offer a lot of choice. You are not a large retailer and people land on your site with the intention of making a purchase. An affiliate marketing site is similar to a popup store that promotes one product instead of a supermarket that offers a lot.

The power of suggestion works better than a ton of choices. A customer will take a liking to a product if you tell them about all that you are offering. Even more so if you have personally tested and have taken a liking to the product. If you offer just one product or a couple of products and you offer it at the best price available then, even if the customer does a quick price comparison, it is likely that such a person will return to your website. Also, if you focus on a single product or business, then it makes it easier to use keywords optimally.

Content is Crucial

You must remember that viewers visit websites to gain information and to be entertained, so you need to make sure that the content you put up on the site is structured around the product that you want to promote. Another point that you must remember is that search engines can tell whether the content on your site is of high quality or not.

High-quality content will rank better in search engine results. It will help increase the traffic to your site and will increase the chances of making sales as well. Your SEO strategy will increase your online visibility, so make it a point to use the top keywords from your blog or site related to the product you are promoting.

A good SEO description along with good content will make your site quite popular. The content that you offer needs to be interesting and engaging. Also, make sure that the content on offer relates to different topics and don't restrict yourself to a single genre. You can attract a larger audience base if you do this. Ensure that the quality of content you are offering is persistent. The subtle power of suggestion certainly works better than bombarding the site with lots of links.

Promote your Site

If you don't promote your site, then how will you get others to know about your website? There are only so many friends who will click on the links and, if you want to land a major gig, you need to promote your site. To do this, you must list your site on popular search engines, write online press releases, and promote your site on different forums and platforms related to your niche. If you have a friend with an extremely popular blog or social media account, you can ask that person to subtly promote your website on their platform.

Don't be invisible or Anonymous

An important rule of online marketing is that you must not stay invisible or anonymous. If you don't have the confidence to market yourself to the world, then don't expect to capture their attention. If you want to be a successful affiliate marketer, then you need to put yourself out there. You need to create a strong online presence for your site.

Becoming an affiliate marketer will help further your goal of earning more than 100k per month. Affiliate marketing can be a great stream of additional income. By following the simple steps given in this chapter, you can become a successful affiliate marketer.

Chapter 7: Grow your Email List

If you want your business to be successful and profitable, then you need to have a huge base of audience you can market to. The easiest way in which you can do this is by email marketing. Before you can get started with email marketing, you need to work on growing your email list. By following the simple steps given in this chapter, you can successfully build your email list.

Offer Something of Value

You need to make sure that you can retain the attention of email recipients. The best way to go about this is to offer them something of value. Something that will not only make them curious but will also add value to their life. Every email recipient will wonder what is in it for them if they open your email and subscribe to your email list. So, make sure that the emails you are sending out offers something of value to the reader and will prompt them to share their email address and subscribe to your email list.

A sign-up Button

Not everyone who reads your emails needs to be a part of your email list. For instance, if you provide your email address on a social media platform, then it isn't necessary that all your followers are present on your email list. Don't forget that people can also share your email with their friends. If you share something valuable in your emails, the chances of the reader sharing the email with their email list increases. To make things easier for visitors, you can add a join my email list link in all your emails.

Sign-Up Form on Your Website

If someone wants to do any business with you, then the first place they will look is your website, so don't miss out on this opportunity to connect with visitors. Please include a sign-up form on your business website so that all those interested will be able to sign up immediately.

At Events

If you host any events that require the attendees to sign up or register in advance, then that's a great way to collect email addresses. In fact, you can collect email addresses without seeming too obvious. Whenever someone registers to be a part of the event you are hosting, then they will invariably share their email address with you and that's the perfect time to include such people in your email list.

Industry Tradeshows

Different industry events, tradeshows, or even conferences are a great place to grow your email list. These events provide you with the opportunity to connect with not just potential customers but also similar businesses, so whenever you attend such an event, don't forget to put up a sign-up list at the conference.

Existing Database

You must never underestimate the power of the

existing list of contacts you have. This database can include all your friends, family members, acquaintances, or even colleagues. In fact, your initial email list might just comprise of all these people. You can encourage them to share your emails with their email lists. It will certainly take a while to grow your email list, but growth is unavoidable. You can obtain their feedback and make the necessary changes to the way you send emails.

Downloadable White Paper

There are a couple of lead magnets that you can use to grow your email list. The simplest way in which you can do this is by offering a lead magnet like a downloadable white paper or any other resource in exchange for the reader's email address. Make sure that the content you are offering is not just unique but is entertaining and informative as well. It must be such that it encourages readers to subscribe to your email list. You can even offer them a sneak peek of the white paper or the other educational resource and they can unlock the rest if they sign up for your email list. It is a simple and effective way to build your email list.

Sign-up with Their Phone

You must make it easy for your existing as well as potential customers to join your email list by enabling them to sign-up for your list using their phones. For instance, you can use a tool like the Text-to-Join tool that Constant Contact offers to let people join your email list by sending them a message along with your business code.

Membership Forms

If you plan on offering subscriptions or memberships, then you must include a sign-up option in such forms. When you include such a form, it will encourage people to sign up and it will not even look like you are trying to gather email addresses.

Social Media

You can always add a sign-up to my email list option on the business pages of your social media accounts. Social media comes in handy if you are trying to increase the reach of your business. If your business has social media accounts, then include a sign-up option on those pages. You can always encourage your followers and fans to subscribe to your email list. If you want this method to work, then you need to post exceptional and interesting content on your profiles. If you can impress the viewer with your profile, then it is quite likely that such a person will sign up for your email list as well.

Facebook ads

You can run Facebook ad campaigns to widen the reach of your business. While you do this, you can use this platform to grow your email list. Instead of using the ads on Facebook to direct the web traffic to a landing page, you can use it to encourage users to sign up for your email list.

Exclusive Access

One of the best ways in which you can grow your email list is by offering something exclusive to the readers. If you can offer something that the audience will find interesting and will not find elsewhere, then it will motivate them to sign up for your email list. It can be something like free shipping on an order, an exclusive discount, or even an exclusive preview to a sale.

Now that you are aware of the different techniques that you can follow to grow your email list, the next step is to implement these tips and grow your email list.

Chapter 8: Email Marketing

Email marketing is a subtle and effective way to coax your subscribers to become paying customers. When done right, email marketing can increase the profitability of your business. If you want your dropshipping business to generate over $100k per month, then you need to work on converting your audience into a paying tribe. To do this, follow the simple strategies given in this section.

Email Marketing Strategies

Now that you have an email list in place, you need to concentrate on email marketing, so what is the most successful email marketing strategy that you can use? Did you know that over 200 billion emails are sent out every day? Well, that's a whole lot of competition that you need to worry about. Also, keep in mind that those email numbers keep increasing every day. Therefore, it is quintessential that you know how to go about email marketing to reach your target audience and retain their attention.

Establish your Goals

You cannot create a marketing campaign without setting certain goals and the same applies to an email marketing campaign as well. If you want to run a successful email marketing campaign, then you need to think about the goals that you want to achieve. Your goal can be to welcome new subscribers, nurture the relationship with existing customers, increase the rate of engagement, re-engage with subscribers, or even segment your subscribers. According to your goals you will be able to design the campaign. Not just that, your goals will also dictate the kind of content you can include in emails.

Types of Emails

You need to understand that there are different types of emails you can send. Usually, they are grouped into three categories and they are promotional emails, relational emails, and transactional emails. Promotional emails are the ones that you will send when you want to inform readers about different promotional offers you are running. The relational emails allow you to give subscribers their weekly updates or any other relevant information that helps maintain good customer relationship. Transactional emails are the ones that you will send if you have to confirm a subscription, confirm an order, or anything related to any transaction related to your business. Transactional emails are the response to any action that the subscriber takes on your website.

Your Audience

If you have been into email marketing for a while, then you will know your audience. If you are just getting started with email marketing, then you will need to take some time to get a general understanding of your audience. You need to understand your audience since this is the primary criterion that describes the kind of content you can use. It is quite easy to gather all the necessary information that you need about your audience. You can use the metrics from social media profiles and Google Analytics to get a general understanding of your audience. These tools will provide you with data about different metrics like the demographics of your audience, their interests, location, and such. Gather all this information and analyze it. When you do this, you will have a rough idea of the kind of content you can create for your emails.

Use Technology

There are different email marketing tools that you can use to create a successful email marketing campaign. When you are selecting a tool to work with, look for something that offers automation, provides templates, and helps with campaign creation. The service you opt for must seamlessly integrate with any other software that you use like WordPress; it must help you segment your audience and must provide you with a good analysis of your campaigns.

Opt-ins

You need to have an email list if you want to run a great campaign, so to attract more people to join your email list, you need to have a bunch of great opt-ins. You need to have an attractive sign-up form that encourages readers to sign up for your email group or subscribe to your emails.

Emails and Follow-ups

Once you are aware of your goals, the type of emails and the audience you need to work with, you need to plan your email marketing campaign. You need to plan the kind of emails you want to send. The content that you will include in your emails is quite important, so don't just send the readers a random template with a generic mail. Instead, you need to spend some time creating an attractive email that makes users stick around and not click on the unsubscribe button. You must not only plan for the emails you want to send, but also think about the follow-up emails to send.

Subject Line

The subject line that you use for your emails is quite important. The subject line is the first thing that the viewer will see, so you need to make sure that it is something that will encourage the reader to open the mail and go through it.

Copy

The next thing that you need to focus on is the email marketing copy you want to use. You need to create a copy that will motivate the reader to read on. It is a good idea to keep the copy short, crisp, and avoid any sales pitches. You need to make the person comfortable before you get down to pitching. It is always a good idea to make the email personalized and the best way to do this is by addressing the subscriber by their name. Also, don't forget to include a call to action in your emails. What is the action that you want the reader to perform after reading the email? The call to action needs to be easy and simple to understand.

Email Marketing Design

If you want to run a successful campaign, then you need to concentrate on the email design. If the email looks terrible, then it will reflect rather badly on your business and it might make the reader stop reading. A lot of people tend to check their emails on their mobile devices, so you need to make sure that your email template is responsive to the device it is being viewed on and can optimize itself immediately.

While writing the copy for your email, make sure that you don't include too many pictures. Usually, most email users tend to disable the images option, and when they do this, the reader cannot view the images you use in your email, so it is a good idea to stick to text.

Test

Sending out your first email is the first step to running a successful email marketing campaign. To optimize the results you receive from this campaign and to improve your future campaigns, you need to collect data. You need to test everything that's a part of your email marketing campaign. It means that you need to test everything from the design of the email, the template you use, the copy you write, subject lines, and the call to actions you use. You must also experiment with different timings and segments of your audience. Gather all the data that you can from all this and keep track of it. After a while, it will help you find the best practices to optimize the results of your email marketing campaign.

Get People to Read Your Emails

All the different strategies that you use for email marketing will not matter if you cannot get people to read your emails. Even if you have an extensive database of email addresses, what good do you think it will do your business if you cannot get anyone to read your emails? Well, the answer is that it does you no good, so in this section you will learn about the different ways in which you can make the reader read your emails.

Deliver value

The emails that you send need to be short and simple to understand. If the emails are lengthy, then you will certainly lose the interest of the reader. With emails it is all about quality and not quantity. You can use the emails to extend any offers to the reader that they will not receive otherwise. A good sales pitch is like a greased slide at a playground; your reader will smoothly slide down without any resistance whatsoever. The opening sentence of the email needs to be short, crisp, and to the point. It needs to pique the reader's curiosity and must make the reader want to read through the email. You need to use your brand voice to convey the information that you want to in a clear and informative manner.

Compelling Subject Line

The subject line of your emails must be such that it compels the reader to open the emails. The subject line needs to be precise and descriptive. The subject line must not bore readers and must not be difficult to understand. When you are crafting the subject line, you can use a couple of the tips given here.

The subject line can include ambiguous statements that make the reader curious. The subject line must address a relevant concern of the subscriber. It needs to show some value or create a sense of urgency. It can perhaps trigger an emotional response with a bold and true claim.

Write the Emails Together

If the email is a part of a drip campaign, then try writing them all at once. If you do this, then you can maintain a consistent style of writing and can avoid any choppy work. You can lead the reader through different stages of a sales funnel smoothly if you write all the emails in one go.

Unicode Symbols

If you want your emails to grab the reader's attention, then you need to make the emails seem personalized. You can use Unicode symbols or even glyphs in the subject line to make it stand out from the other emails in their inbox. You need to use these symbols carefully, because if you overuse them it will make the emails seem rather gimmicky.

The Timing Matters

It isn't just about the content that you send your subscribers; the time at which you send the emails matters as well. If you send the emails during off hours, it is quite likely that the subscriber will think about opening it later and will ultimately forget about it, so the best time to send emails is around mid-morning or during the afternoon. Try to avoid lunch hours.

Follow these simple tips while drafting your emails to make sure that the reader reads them like you intended!

Chapter 9: Facebook Advertising

We love giving our hands and arms sufficient rest, and this is not only in the dropshipping business. We choose home delivery over takeaway, online ticket booking over standing in queue to book a ticket, and online shopping over walking to a physical store and making a purchase. It is for this reason that you must advertise on Facebook if you want to have a successful dropshipping business. Facebook is the perfect platform to highlight your products since there are 1.23 billion active users every month. These users will click, like, or view your page while they stalk their crush without their knowledge. What else can you ask for?

If you have some knowledge about online marketing, you know that it takes time to improve your ranking on a social media page. Facebook advertisements will help you get your sales up while you continue to build your SEO game. When you market your business, your goal is obvious. You only want to increase the traffic on your page and maximize the number of products you sell. When the goal or objective of your advertisement is clear, Facebook will win the race.

Unlike other websites, Facebook allows you to post any promotional and sponsored posts along with its normal newsfeed. You can also post separate sponsored advertisements. What do you think happens here? When you generate paid advertisements for your website, users will go through the advertisements. This is because the advertisement is shown along with the newsfeed. Facebook will also show you the number of comments that are against the latest version of the post that the users are viewing. You must remember that it is the first impression that matters.

Structure of Facebook Advertisements

There are three stages to advertising on Facebook.

1. Campaigns

2. Advertisement sets that you launch for a targeted audience

3. Advertisements

Campaigns

This is the stage where you need to define the objectives of your advertisement. Let us assume that you have two types of advertisement sets for your website – one is for the full website and the other is for specific products. You have certain objectives for both sets of advertisements. With the first type of advertisement, your objective is to:

Maximize the traffic to your website

Obtaining more likes

Increasing the base for your business

Include some offers

Increasing general awareness of the brand

Maximize the independent sales of the products

It is at this stage that you need to categorize every product carefully and create or build the right campaign for the different categories.

Advertisement Sets

In this stage, you need to develop advertisements based on your audience's interest, demography, occupation, types of posts they read, pages they have commented on, their purchasing frequency, personal interest, and their life events. You can use a tool called 'Facebook Audience Insights' to make this process easier. You need to use this tool if you want to make an advertisement that will generate revenue. For instance, if you sell sports accessories, you must develop different advertisements for your customized audience, a set for people who have purchased from your website and for the people who live close to your store.

Advertisements

This is the final stage. An advertisement is the most relevant and narrowest combination of the targeted audience and the most useful objective. This is where you will create your live advertisement. For every part of the advertisement set, you must mix and match different descriptions, images, and multiple logos. You can then use these combinations to see which one will work best. You must always remember to run the A/B tests. A simple change in image or color can boost the rates by at least 90 percent.

How to Target the Right Audience

Studies show that if you do not target the right audience, you will run your dropshipping business into the ground. If you have conducted sufficient research on the dropshipping business, you know that your audience matters.

Interest, Occupation and Demography

It is obvious that an eighty-year-old man and a high school girl will not like the same Facebook pages. You can use 'Facebook Audience Insight' to distinguish your target audience by using their occupation, age, recent life events, hobbies, purchasing frequency, and interests. Your audience's interests include the types of posts they like, the groups they belong to, and the pages they visit.

If your company sells kitchen appliances, Facebook will target the users in the same area who have recently purchased kitchen appliances. It will also give you a list of people who have some interest in kitchen appliances. You can then target the potential customers. This is what you need if you want to establish a dropshipping store.

Geography

When your circle is concentrated, you will succeed in the dropshipping business. When you advertise your products on Facebook, you must first start with the location. If you are a retailer in Asia, you cannot expect to sell products in Australia unless you start an online store. You must always target potential buyers in the areas where you know you can deliver products on time.

Custom Audiences

Apart from posting your advertisements to targeted audiences, you can also customize your viewer list. You can obtain the email addresses of your viewers from positive reviewers, previous customers, and people who have contacted you for specific products.

Budget

It is true that money matters. You do not want to waste a single penny when you are starting a dropshipping business. Experts suggest that you always go slow. Instead of investing a large sum of money in your business at a single time, you must only campaign a small amount of money. You must follow the growth and then invest accordingly. If you use the 'Facebook Advertising Tool,' you can either make a one-time investment or pay for advertisements daily. You must always test new things. You will lose some money initially, but you will make more money than you will lose. You must learn the lessons and remember that you must only focus on marketing. You do not have to worry about packaging, inventory, or shipping. You must pull your socks up and try new things. You must not worry if you lose some money. It is true that the daily budget is lower for obvious reasons, but experts recommend that you go for the 'Lifetime Budget' until you learn how to invest. When you pay daily, you will spend more when compared to the amount you spend on the 'Lifetime Budget.' It is a good idea to choose the lifetime budget if you want Facebook to spend the money you have invested only on advertisements. Facebook will spend your money in the following ways: on the basis of impressions (CPM) or clicks (CPC). With the CPC, Facebook will generate advertisements for you and target relevant users. With the CPM, Facebook will deduct money from your investment when someone clicks your advertisement at least a thousand times. The 'Facebook Advertising Tool' will allow you to include any other discount coupon if you want.

You can place your advertisement on Facebook in the following order:

Desktop News Feed

Mobile News Feed

Instagram

Audience Network

Desktop Right Column

Statistics show that the first two options always generate the maximum amount of traffic. This means that you must avoid the desktop right column.

Creating and optimizing Ads

Facebook offers multiple advertising options and you don't always have to promote a single post. You can select the type of ad based on different objectives. One of these objectives can be to boost or promote a specific post. There are different options that include promoting your Facebook page, directing others to your dropshipping website, increasing the rate of conversion and also encourage users to claim any offer that you provide. Once you select the objective of your campaign, then you can select different options regarding the targeted audience, budget, and the creatives that you want to use for your ads. If you select an objective, it will help meet your advertising goals. There are three placement options available and they are your desktop feed, the column on the right side of the screen, and the mobile newsfeed. The default option is that all these three options will be selected. If you don't want your ad to be displayed in any of these locations, then you need to click on the remove button that's present next to the location name. Usually, people tend to spend a lot of their time and money on Facebook Ads without understanding the way it works. If you want to avoid doing this, then you need to ensure that the ads perform according to the objectives that you have set for yourself.

In this section, you will learn about the various things that you can do to create and optimize the Facebook Ads you create.

Appropriate Editor

Ads Manager and the Power Editor are the two tools that Facebook offers to create ads. When you are trying to decide between these two options, you need to consider the size of your business and the number of ads you want to run at any given point of time. The Ads Manager option usually suits the needs of most businesses. If you are a large advertiser and want to have precise control over all your campaigns, then you must opt for the Power Editor tool.

Objective

The Facebook Ads Manager helps you design an advertising campaign, but you need to set some objectives for this tool to effectively fulfill this objective. There are ten pre-installed objectives that you can choose from and they include clicks to website, page likes, app installations, app engagement, website conversions, page post engagement, video views, offer claims, event responses, and local awareness. Whenever you select an objective from this section, it helps Facebook serve your needs better and improves the overall efficiency of your advertising campaign. If you want to increase the traffic to your website, then merely click on that option from the list of objectives. Once you do this, then Facebook will ask you for the URL that you want to promote. If you want to use any automated marketing software, then you need to ensure that you are using URL and UTM parameters to track the traffic as well as conversions.

Select your Audience

If you are using Facebook ads for the first time, then you will need to try a couple of different targeting options until you find one that works well for you. Facebook offers different targeting criteria that you can use. If you are not too sure about the kind of audience you must target, then take some time to think about your objectives. If you want to increase traffic to your website, then you must focus on all those who will be interested in what you are offering. If you want to build awareness of your business, then it makes sense to create an ad that will appeal to the general audience. The different factors that you must consider while creating an ad are the location, gender, age, interest, language, finances, life events, behaviors, connections, and work of the audience.

You also have the option to select a custom audience. If you opt for a custom audience, then it gives you the option to target all those present on your business's contact list like the people who visit your website or app users. Once you find a group that you think will react favorably to your ads, then the next step is to save that selected audience.

Budget

There are two types of budget that Facebook offers for its ads and they are the daily and lifetime budgets. If you want to run an ad continuously throughout the day, then you must opt for the daily budget option. By using this option, Facebook will pace your daily budget according to the number of times you want the ad to be displayed. The minimum budget that you can set is $1 per day. If you want to create an ad that will run for a specific period of time, then you must opt for the lifetime budget option. Facebook will pace the entire budget of the ad according to the lifecycle of the ad. You must decide the schedule for the ad. For instance, do you want the ad to run immediately or do you want it to run during a specific period? You have the option to customize the ad so that it runs only during a specific hour in any day.

You must select if you want to bid for your objective, clicks, and impressions or not. The way the ad will be displayed is based on this decision. When you do this, you will only pay for a specific ad that will be shown to your target audience. Facebook tends to control your maximum bid when you are using Facebook ads, or it does so usually. If you don't want this, then you must opt or manual bidding. This option gives you free rein over the amount that you want to spend per action that is complete. You must also select the delivery option. There are two delivery options available and they are standard and accelerated delivery. If you want your ad to be shown throughout the day, then opt for standard delivery. If you want your ad to reach your target audience quickly, especially if the content of the ad is time-sensitive, then opt for the accelerated delivery option.

Create the ad

How do you think the final ad will look like? Well, it all depends on the objectives that you have set for the ad campaign. If your aim is to increase the web traffic to your website, then Facebook's Ad Manager will suggest the option of "click to website" ads. There are two formats in which you can run this ad and they are Links and Carousels. It means that you can either display one image ads with links to your website or display multiple images in the carousel format. Once you decide the ad format, you must upload your creative assets to it. It is critical that you ensure that you follow the specifications given by Facebook for various ads. For instance, the text that you can use for a single-image ad needs to be less than 90 characters, the link title cannot exceed 25 characters, the image size must be 1200 pixels X 627 pixels and the image ratio is 1:9:1. If you want the images to appear on the News Feed, then the image width needs to be at least 600 pixels.

For a Carousel ad, the recommended image size is 600x600 pixels, the image ratio of 1:1, the text limit is 90 characters, the headline limit is 40 characters, the link description is restricted to 20 characters, and the images you use cannot include more than 20% text.

Report

Even if the ad is up and running, your work goes on. You must observe the performance of the ad. You can use marketing software of your choice or Facebook Ad's Manager to view the results of the ad's performance. If you use Facebook Ad's Manager, then the dashboard will give you the necessary insights about the way the campaign is working. The dashboard will show you information like the costs incurred per day. The dashboard is organized into columns that make it easy to filter the different metrics that you will want to look at like the performance, engagement rate, videos, apps, clicks, and the other settings. Apart from Facebook Ads Manager the other tools you can use are Hootsuite Ads, Qwaya,

AdEspresso, AdSpring, PerfectAudience, AdRoll, and Driftrock.

Always use Audience Targeting

If you don't have any specific form of targeting in mind, then it can be quite a tedious job to advertise to a general audience. In fact, it is effectively a recipe for failure. It will be a waste of your time and resources if you run an advertising campaign without a targeted audience. There are multiple targeting options that you can choose from and make sure that you explore these options to create an ad campaign that is effective.

Content Placement

If the content is placed at the beginning and at the end of the ad, it is quite likely that a lot of users will not view the content. Therefore, it is imperative that the content you want to promote is placed strategically. The content that you include can be a link or even a call to action button. You must always use a strong call to action that lets users know about the specific action that you want them to take. You don't always need a directive. Instead of merely telling them to do something, give them the reasons for why they need to do a specific thing. Try to be convincing and persuasive instead of merely being directive.

Rotating the Ad

If you are using specific targeting for your ads, then you will need to keep advertising to the small audience repeatedly. It means that you will need to change the content that you display in your ads every week or so. If you keep using the same content repeatedly for the ads, it is quite likely that the viewer will skip your ad. You can use conversions of pixels to track whether the ads are effective or not.

Tips to Create a Great Facebook Advertisement Campaign

There are many social networking platforms that

you can use to advertise your products. Each of these platforms has its own integrated system for advertising. Facebook is still one of the best platforms to use since there are many insights and features you can use to create the best advertisements. You also have a large audience. This means that you must start off with advertising on Facebook when you start a new company. This does not mean that every brand knows how to use Facebook effectively for marketing. There are many people who throw their money down the drain because they do not know how to use the different features. They also do not have a strategy. I sincerely hope that that is not you. You must know what the best practices are if you want to effectively use Facebook to market your products.

This section lists five tips that you can use to create a killer Facebook advertisement.

Always Mine Your Audience's Insights

Facebook offers a tool called 'Facebook's

Audience Insights,' and this is the best tool an entrepreneur can use. This tool allows you to learn more about your audience before you risk your budget. It also helps to ensure that you do not lose your targeted audience. This tool mines the data available on Facebook and shows you who your target market is. This information is based on the people who have already look at your page.

You will know exactly which user you need to contact, which user will follow your page, and which user will follow through and make a purchase. This will save you a lot of money and will give you sufficient time to focus on the quality of your advertisement.

Create Unique Advertisements for Different Audiences

You can create separate advertisements for your target audience when you use Facebook to market your products. This means that you can create different advertisements and deliver them to different addresses. Alternatively, you can create the exact advertisement and deliver it to different addresses. The result is to learn who to target.

Let us assume that you are a retailer and you sell sports accessories. You may have different shoes that you want to market to different groups. You can create two different advertisements and deliver those advertisements to different target markets. You can target the first advertisement towards professional sports players while targeting the second advertisement towards college or school sports players. The advertisements will be different, but you are pushing your audience to consider purchasing the same item.

Accompany Advertisement with Landing Pages

You must always push visitors through the landing page before you link an advertisement with a product page or your website. A landing page will allow you to maximize your advertising efforts before you ask your users to purchase those products. It is best to have a landing page since Facebook advertising is not cheap. You have to learn how to spend money on the clicks and learn to make every click count. If you send them to a landing page without giving them sufficient knowledge or information about what they must do next, it is a waste of money.

Use Striking Imagery

You will hear people tell you how you must write Facebook copy or develop an advertisement. For some reason, people do not focus on the images they use in advertisements. This is bad since the visual content has more influence on the individual than textual content.

You do not have to use an image of your product, service, or business. It is a good idea to use a relevant image that will catch a person's eye and make them want to read your advertisement. Facebook will tell you that you cannot use any image that has at least twenty percent words. Therefore, it is important to remember that you must use an image to grab your target's attention and not display any message. You must take advantage of this in your advertisement.

Establish a Budget and Bid Strategy

It is important that you set up a budget and bid strategy. Otherwise, you will end up spending more money than you wanted. Facebook makes this easier for you since it allows you to use a tool known as 'Optimized CPM.' If you use this tool, you give Facebook permission to bid for an advertisement space using the goals and constraints you provide. This allows you to maximize your budget and avoid spending too much on an advertisement. When you know how much an advertisement space costs and know how to allocate your budget, you must let Facebook take care of the campaign.

When you want to create a killer Facebook advertisement campaign, you must understand the platform and the features that you can use. You first need to focus on the platform you are using before you worry about the advertisement. When you determine who your target audience is and how much you are willing to spend on the advertisement, you can focus on the finer details. You can use these five tips to start to experience initial success. You must remember that Facebook changes its advertising platform constantly, so you must stay on top of learning new things every day. You must also know how to apply your learning when you develop an advertisement. By following these simple steps, you can increase the visibility and online reach of your business. When this happens, you can convert your audience into a paying tribe and this in turn will help you achieve your financial objectives.

Chapter 10: Google AdWords

Google AdWords is another effective marketing tool that you can use to promote and market your dropshipping business online. You need to increase the online visibility of your business if you want to attract potential customers. Doing this is necessary to increase the profitability quotient of your business.

Four Surprising Ways to Use Google AdWords

There is a legend in the world of digital marketing. A college graduate was applying for a job at all the large corporations in the country, but he never heard back from those companies. He then used Google AdWords to bid on the different executives at these large companies. When these executives looked for themselves on Google, they found a paid search advertisement. When they clicked on that advertisement, they landed on the graduate's resume. These executives were impressed and peeved and decided to offer the graduate a job. This is an inventive use of AdWords, isn't it?

This example shows that you can use Google AdWords in any way you want. Most business owners believe that they can use Google AdWords to bid on keywords that have a commercial intent. They then use these keywords to convince potential customers to click on the advertisement to visit your website. For example, a baker may bid for keywords like "chocolate cake" and "mini muffin," while a psychologist may bid for keywords like "mental illness" or "depression." They use the classic cost-per-click advertising, and this is a great way to allocate the budget.

The only problem with Google AdWords is that it can become very expensive when your competitors begin to bid on the same keywords as you. Fortunately, you do not have to use Google AdWords only for this purpose. There are multiple ways to use Google AdWords, and this chapter lists some of the most unusual ways of using Google AdWords to advertise your products and services.

Poaching Your Competitor's Clients

Most customers will Google the vendor or retailer before they make a purchase. This is because they want to compare different vendors and see where they can get the best deal. What if your customer does not choose your business to make that purchase? You do not have to worry. All you need to do is find a way to intercept your customers during this phase of research. Instead of focusing only on the keywords and bidding on them, you must try to set your advertisements using brand names of some well-established customers. When you insert your business into their conversation this way, you can sway the customers who are on the fence. If you think this is not ethically sound, you must know that this is common practice. For instance, if you visit the platform 'Outbrain,' you will find an advertisement from 'Taboola,' which is one of its competitors. If you were to search for 'Taboola,' you will find an advertisement from 'Outbrain.'

Target Customers Who Are Not Ready to Buy Yet

This sounds a little counterintuitive doesn't it? Why must you go after people who have no idea if they want to purchase your product or not? John Leo Weber, who is the VP of marketing at Projectmanager.com, has said that this always boils down to how you interpret the value that Google AdWords provides. Advertisers often bid on the keywords that have a high buyer intent. This is because they believe that AdWords is a conversion engine. That is where they are wrong. It is important for an advertiser to know that AdWords is a traffic engine. As an advertiser, you can bid on keywords that have lower buyer intent. This will help to increase the number of people who visit your website. If you continue with this mindset, you will begin to identify a non-conversion as an opportunity and not as a loss. When you have specific marketing funnels in place, you can capture your leads and nurture them into doing what you want them to do. You can increase your customer base at half or one-fourth of the cost. You can then use these marketing funnels to convert the leads into customers. In other words, you can remarket your product with a twist. Instead of paying Google or any other platform fifty dollars for a click on a keyword, you, as an advertiser, must use this tactic to market your products.

Identify the People You Are Not Selling To

Let us look at the following example – if you sell software that will help physicians manage their practices, you know that your product cannot be used by medium or large healthcare systems. Therefore, you will not approach them to be your customer. When you use keywords like "medical management software" or "medical office software" you will identify your target audience. This is great, but there are some people who want to support and manage their large practices. Beth

Cooper, the Marketing Manager at KNB Communications, mentioned that you couldn't sell your product to every person in your customer base regardless of how great the product is. The trick is to define your set of keywords that these people will not look for. You can add them as 'negative keywords' if you use AdWords to market your product. This means that the people using those keywords will never see your advertisement. Going back to our example, if you tell AdWords that keywords like "large" and "hospital" are negative words, you can remove customers who only want the tool for a large corporation. You can also remove keywords like "free" and "open source" since the client does not want to pay for clicks.

You may wonder why all this information is important. You need to understand that negative keywords save you a lot of money. In an AdWords campaign, you pay for a click. You certainly do not want to pay for a person who is not going to be your customer. When you target your campaign, you will receive decent revenue.

When you use negative keywords, Google will assign each advertisement a better score. If there is a better score, the advertisement will have a higher ranking, which will increase the number of clicks.

Support Your Organic Initiatives

According to data collected in 2017, customers only click on Google advertisements about fifteen percent of the time. The other customers look at search results that are not an advertisement. It is for this reason that search engine optimization is a cornerstone of digital marketing. When you create valuable content and optimize the content to ensure that it ranks well when compared to other advertisements. When you use the right keywords, Google will rank your website which will increase the number of clicks you receive on your advertisement. This also means that you will no longer have to pay a large sum of money every time someone clicks on your advertisement. It does take time to write content that can attract an individual. It can also take two or three months before you see the results of your SEO campaign, so what must you do to understand which keywords you must use before you spend weeks and months on optimizing, writing, building backlinks, and generating traffic? This is where Google AdWords comes in. Elliot Brown, a marketing and SEO consultant, said that AdWords data is invaluable for any keyword research. If you know that some keywords are generating traffic, you can generate traffic for your website for free using those keywords. It may take days, weeks, or months to move organic results higher in a customer's search. You will, however, see the results of your pay-per-click campaigns when you launch the campaign. It takes less time to develop an advertisement on AdWords than it takes to develop content for a blog.

When you determine which keywords are effective in driving traffic to your page or website, you must double back and include those keywords in your strategy. You must also remember to share the AdWords data with the team in your business that deals with generating organic traffic. When you do this, you align everyone's effort around the keywords for your business. When you have determined the keywords, and know how to incorporate those keywords when you generate new content, you must use Google AdWords to drive traffic to your website.

Pay-per-click advertisements will not increase the organic ranking of your advertisement. Money can never do that for you. A pay-per-click advertisement, however, can act as a catalyst and increase the traffic on your website. These advertisements also allow Google to place your website as an option when someone searches for something relevant. This will increase the number of times your website comes up in a search.

Launch a Google AdWords Campaign

Google AdWords is one of the best advertising

platforms these days if you want to advertise your products and attract potential customers quickly. In this section, you will learn different tips that you can follow to launch a successful Google AdWords campaign for your business.

Account Structure

If you want your ad to be profitable, then you will need a well-structured Google AdWords account. A well-structured account will help with relevancy. You can reduce your cost per acquisition by improving the structure of your AdWords account. You must make sure that the keywords and the ad groups in all your campaigns are closely related to one another. If you do this, then your reward is that Google will reduce your advertising costs. You need to ensure that even when you run multiple campaigns, the keywords you use along with the ads and the ad group needs to have a consistent theme throughout.

Understand AdWords

Before you think about using AdWords for marketing, you must understand the strengths and weaknesses of this method of advertising. AdWords is a great option if you have a highly targeted campaign that will help generate measurable and rapid results. If you want to improve the generation of leads and sales, then this is a good tool. You must also understand that using Google AdWords is not a one-time investment and it needs recurring investment. If you are looking for brand awareness, then this isn't the most ideal platform for you. In fact, it is quite difficult to track the metrics related to brand awareness on this platform. Whenever you are designing an advertising campaign, you need to consider the strengths and the weaknesses of the platform that you want to use, if you want the campaign to be effective.

Target Audience

You need to research and understand your target

audience if you want the AdWords campaign to be successful. It will take a while for you to understand your audience and dedicate the necessary time and resources necessary to do this. Take a look at the different types of websites your target audience spends their time on, the language, the content they present, and their ad campaigns. You can use AdWords to research about all this and it doesn't cost you a dime.

Specific Goal

Every campaign that you design needs to have a specific goal and you must not combine them. It is quite easy to get overambitious while designing an AdWords campaign. It is important that you set only one specific goal for every campaign. If you do this, it will also improve the ROI of the campaign.

Targeted Landing Page

A common mistake that people who are using AdWords make is that they target the traffic from their ads to their homepages. Most of the time, people tend to invest a lot of money in ads and notice that they don't get any results. It is mainly because they don't direct the traffic to the appropriate pages. Directing web traffic to a homepage is a bad idea. Take a moment to think about it. Whenever someone uses Google to search for something, they are looking for something specific. If you direct them to a homepage, they will be met with a dozen elements and options and they will need to spend some more time to search for what they are looking for. Instead, you must create a targeted landing page to lead the traffic to. After all, as a business owner your aim is conversion. What better way to do this than to direct the traffic to the specific page displaying the specific thing that they are looking for?

Ad Copy

Before you can start an AdWords campaign, you must create different versions of the ad copy. Try to produce at least ten versions of the ad copy. A couple of slight changes are all that's necessary to improve the conversion rates. If you have multiple versions of an ad, then you can test them all to see which copy generates the best results. You need to divide your budget into smaller segments and test it for each copy of the ad. The data that you gather from doing this will help you find the most successful version of the ad. Once you have this, then you can allocate a bigger budget to run that campaign.

ROI

When you run a campaign, you will obviously have some specific goals. Once your campaign is up and running, you need to generate whether you are able to generate any positive ROI or not. It is quite simple to calculate this.

You can compare this cost to the profit model that you have in mind: it can be the profit margin on a product or the estimated lifetime value of one customer for your business.

Test

While using AdWords, you must remember that your work never really ends. Even when the campaign is up and running, you will need to make some change or other. Small variations in your ad copy, the keywords you use, the landing page you direct visitors to, and pretty much anything else that you can think of. Make these changes and you will notice some change in the ROI. Keep making these simple changes to improve the efficiency of your campaign.

Budget

If you are just getting started with AdWords, then you need to make sure that you keep your daily budget low, at least initially. It is quite difficult to determine the amount of traffic your ads will generate and how quickly you will spend your budget. The last thing that you want to do is blow your marketing budget on a tool that doesn't give you any positive ROI, so start with a small budget and see how it goes before you expand your budget.

Ad Copy

You must not forget that the ad copy and the images you use matter a lot when it comes to AdWords. In fact, these two things are necessary to attract the right business prospects. Content is King and it will do you good to remember this simple rule. You can even split-test two versions of the ad to see which of the ads does better. The images that you use for your ads must grab the attention of the viewer and must prompt them to click on your ad.

Conclusion

I want to thank you once again for choosing this book. I hope it proved to be an informative and enjoyable read.

Dropshipping is a relatively new business concept. There are different changes that constantly keep taking place in this business model, so it is important that you keep up with all the latest trends as well as business practices. In this book, you were provided with all the necessary information that you need to launch your dropshipping business. If you have any doubts, then please refer to the concerned chapter in this book. You must make it a point to soak up as much information about this business model as you can if you want to be a successful entrepreneur.

Now, all that you need to do is get started immediately. In the words of the wise Master Oogway from Kung-Fu Panda, "Today is a gift and that's why it's known as the present." So, there is no time like the present to get started. The idea of starting a business on your own can be a little daunting. You need to gather your courage and take the first step. If you put in the necessary hard work, dedicate your time and be a little patient, you can become the owner of a successful business.

It is quite unfortunate that a lot of businesses tend to fail in their first year. If you don't want to be amongst them, then you need the necessary motivation and determination to succeed. Failure is part and parcel of life. Learn from the mistakes you face, and you can overcome any hurdle that comes your way. It is not easy to succeed, have no qualms about it, but once you do, there is nothing that can replicate the high of success.

Take everything that comes your way in your stride and treat it as a learning experience. With the right mindset, there is little that you cannot achieve, so all that you need to do now is to get started.

All the best for your future endeavors!

CPSIA information can be obtained
at www.ICGtesting.com
Printed in the USA
BVHW030125131219
566560BV00001B/47/P